Everyday Life:
EXPLORATION
& DISCOVERY

WALTER A. HAZEN

A GOOD YEAR BOOK™

GOOD YEAR BOOKS
Tucson, Arizona

Photo Credits

Front and back cover, Background; Bridgeman Art Library. Front cover: t. SuperStock: b.r. The Granger Collection. 2: Ancient Greece, Lauros/Giraudon/Bridgeman Art Library. 4: Viking Warrior The Granger Collection, New York. 5: Leif Ericson Ubiquitous/Corbis. 10: The Granger Collection, New York. 12: t Kublai Khan North Wind Picture Archives, b The Granger Collection, New York. 13: The Granger Collection, New York. 18: The Granger Collection, New York. 19: The Granger Collection, New York. 20: The Granger Collection, New York. 21: The Granger Collection, New York. 26: Private Collection, Bonhams, London, UK/Bridgeman Art Library 28: Araldo de Luca/Corbis. 29: Werner Forman/Corbis. 35: Prince Henry Navigator Corbis. 36: Vasco de Gama The Granger Collection, New York. 42: The Granger Collection, New York. 44: The Granger Collection, New York. 45: The Granger Collection, New York. 50: Cortez Saldana/ Museo Nacional de Historia, Mexico City, Mexico/Bridgeman Art Library. 51: Free Agents Limited/Corbis. 52: Granger Collection, New York. 58: Fort Caroline Archivo Iconografico, S.A./Corbis. 60: British Library, London, UK/Bridgeman Art Library. 61: North Wind Picture Archives. 66: North Wind Picture Archives. 67: North Wind Picture Archives. 68: The Granger Collection, New York. 74: Stock Montage/ SuperStock. 76: Lee Snider, Photo Images/Corbis. 77: North Wind Picture Archives. 82: The Granger Collection, New York. 83: Archivo Iconografico, S.A./ Corbis. 85: The Granger Collection, New York

Dedication

To Martha, Jordan, and Allison.

Acknowledgments

Grateful acknowledgment is extended to Roberta Dempsey, Editorial Director at Good Year Books, who patiently guided me through this addition to the "Everyday Life series. Without her advice and support, this book would not have been possible.

I would also like to thank Helen Fisher, Publisher at Good Year Books for giving me the opportunity to continue the "Everyday Life" series. Her support and confidence in me is likewise appreciated.

Good Year Books

are available for most basic curriculum subjects plus many enrichment areas. For more Good Year Books, contact your local bookseller or educational dealer. For a complete catalog with information about other Good Year Books, please contact:

Good Year Books
P. O. Box 91858
Tucson, Arizona 85752
1-800-511-1530
www.goodyearbooks.com

Editor: Roberta Dempsey
Cover Design: Ronan Design
Interior Design: Dan Miedaner

Copyright © 2005 Good Year Books.

Printed in the United States of America.

ISBN: 1-59647-010-0

1 2 3 4 5 6 7 8 9 - - 07 06 05 04

Table of Contents

Table of Contents *continued*

From *Everyday Life: Exploration and Discovery* © 2005 Good Year Books.

Introduction

By the early 1400s, European civilization, which had been mired in the doldrums of the Middle Ages for almost 1,000 years, had slowly begun to change. Feudalism had ended for the most part, and strong national governments were beginning to emerge. In addition, the Italian Renaissance, with its emphasis on the present rather than the hereafter, was in full bloom. Although no one at the time used such terms, Europe was passing from the Middle Ages into Modern Times.

Another event that marked the beginning of modern history was the great Age of Exploration and Discovery, which began in the mid-1400s and continued almost to the end of the 1600s. Driven by the desire to find an all-water route to Asia, European nations engaged in a race to dominate world trade and foreign markets. Spain carved out a vast empire in the New World from Florida southward into Central and South America. Portugal took control of Brazil and acquired ports and trading posts in India and Africa. France laid claim to land in Canada and in the areas of the Great Lakes and Mississippi River. The Dutch seized the Spice Islands in the East Indies and established settlements in what later became New York and Delaware. Finally, the English founded what in time became the 13 original English colonies along the Atlantic Seaboard in North America.

Each chapter of this book is followed by four pages of activities. Some test a student's ability to think creatively; others measure skills in math, vocabulary, and other subject areas. In addition, the book includes numerous arts-and-crafts activities, and there are even a few puzzles. Students should find *Everyday Life: Exploration and Discovery* enjoyable.

Walter A. Hazen

CHAPTER I

Early Explorations

Europeans in the 1400s did not just decide that they were bored with their humdrum existence and therefore strike off to explore distant horizons. On the contrary, since the beginning of time people have probably wondered what lay just over the next hill or waterway. They would not be human if they did not.

Among the first seafarers and explorers were the Minoans, or Cretans. They established a highly developed civilization on the island of Crete in the Mediterranean some 3,000 years before the birth of Christ. How advanced were the Minoans? Advanced enough to have running water, baths, and toilets that flushed. Compare this to Europeans of the Middle Ages, who used chamber pots and bathed in wooden tubs, if they bathed at all.

Ancient ruins on the island of Crete.

During the height of their existence, the Minoans sailed southeast some 200 miles and established a flourishing trade with Egypt. This trade provided the wealth that made Crete a Mediterranean power for many years. Minoan civilization flourished until about 1400 B.C., when its capital city, Knossos, was destroyed in an earthquake. At about the same time, the island of Crete was overrun by barbaric invaders from the north. These invaders would in time become the Greeks.

The next ancient people to explore distant lands were the Phoenicians. Phoenicia, which controlled the Mediterranean world from 1000 to 700 B.C., was located where Lebanon and western Syria are today. Phoenician sailors became great traders and colonizers. They established colonies on the shores of the Mediterranean in north Africa, Spain, and Sicily. Their greatest colony was Carthage in north Africa, which in time rivaled Rome for supremacy in the Mediterranean. It was the Phoenicians who helped spread the culture and learning of Egypt and Mesopotamia into what later became Europe.

In 470 B.C., the Phoenician colony of Carthage sent General Hanno, a statesman and navigator, to explore Africa's west coast and found colonies there. Leading what must have been the greatest expedition up to that time, Hanno set sail with some 60 galleys packed with more than 30,000 men. All went well at first. Groups of men disembarked along the way and established settlements in northwest Africa, as well as the upper portion of west Africa. But when Hanno reached the Senegal River area at the center of the western coast, his string of uncontested landings came to an end.

When Hanno sent a landing party ashore to look over this newly selected spot, his men were set upon by screaming natives, who pelted the invaders with rocks and stones. Hanno and his men beat back the natives and hastily constructed a camp. Their attempt at founding a colony was doomed, however. The constant beat of native tom-toms and the menacing growls of wild animals kept the Carthaginians on edge. The crowning blow came one morning when a large group of screaming gorillas accosted the camp, terrifying the inhabitants, who believed the beasts to be a race of huge savages. (Hanno later reported that his men captured some of the "women" but that the "men" got away.) This confrontation with the gorillas was enough to make Hanno and his group dash for their ships and return to Carthage in record time.

At about the same time that Hanno was attempting to establish settlements for Carthage, a Greek writer named Herodotus was making his own mark, as a historian and world traveler. Herodotus traveled widely through the Middle East and north Africa, recording what he had seen in such places as Babylon, Egypt, Syria, and Palestine. He also visited Italy and parts of northern Europe. He further added to the geographical knowledge of the day by confirming that the Black and Caspian seas were enclosed bodies of water. Because of his detailed history of the Persian Wars between Persia and the Greeks, Herodotus is known as the "Father of History."

An important explorer of this time period was Alexander the Great, although he is known more for his conquests than his explorations. From 336 to 323 B.C., he conquered most of the known world. His vast empire extended more than 3,000 miles from his native Macedonia to the Indus River in India. Included within this vast realm were the Greek city-states, Egypt, Mesopotamia, and the huge Persian Empire, the conquest of which Alexander completed in 331 B.C. Wherever Alexander went, he built great cities and spread Greek culture. He also sent back information on the lands he explored and conquered to his old tutor Aristotle, one of ancient Greece's greatest philosophers.

Of all ancient peoples, the Romans were the least interested in exploration and discovery. This was no doubt due to their having such a large empire to control and administer. But they did have their moments. A Roman navigator named Hippalus sailed from the Red Sea to the southwest coast of India. More importantly, he was the first to discover that winds known as monsoon winds blew toward India during the winter and Africa during the summer. This knowledge made trips to and from India considerably shorter. Roman traders also reached Ceylon and discovered Cochin China (now part of Vietnam) sometime during the second century A.D.

Perhaps the bravest of early explorers were the Vikings. The Vikings lived in northern Europe, in what later became the Scandinavian countries of Norway, Denmark, and Sweden. In the 800s and 900s they spread terror throughout Europe, raiding and pillaging coastal villages from France to Russia. Then, near the end of the 900s, they crossed the Atlantic and became the first explorers to touch land in North America.

A Viking warrior. The Vikings spread terror throughout Europe in the ninth and tenth centuries.

The first Viking expedition to sail west across the Atlantic was led by Eric the Red. Eric, whose real name was Eric Thorwaldson, was a Norseman, or native of Norway. In 985, he crossed the Atlantic and set foot on a large island in the Arctic Circle off the east coast of Canada. He named the island Greenland because it was so green. The settlements Eric founded there lasted for some 400 years, after which the inhabitants either died out or returned to Norway. Today, Greenland, the world's largest island at 840,000 square miles, is a possession of Denmark.

About the year 1000, Eric the Red's son, Leif Ericson, became the first explorer to touch land in what later became the United States. Therefore, it could be argued that he and not Christopher Columbus discovered the New World. In any event, Leif left Greenland and discovered Newfoundland, after which he proceeded along the coast to what is now Massachusetts. Some

From *Everyday Life: Exploration and Discovery* © 2005 Good Year Books.

historians believe that he may have sailed as far south as New Jersey and Virginia. Leif called the lands he visited Vinland because of the grapes he found growing there. In some historic chronicles, Vinland is referred to as Vineland or Wineland.

Leif Ericson stayed in Vinland for a few months, marveling at the fertile countryside. He then returned to Greenland, where the tales he told of a "new and rich country" stirred interest in further exploration. As a result, the Vikings made two attempts to colonize Vinland. The first might have succeeded except for a freak occurrence. After initially getting along well with the natives of the region, Viking sagas relate that one day a bull got loose and attacked a group of Indians. The Indians viewed this occurrence as an unfriendly act on the part of the Vikings, whereupon they made war on their previously welcomed visitors. Hopelessly outnumbered, the Vikings had no choice but to retreat and leave the island.

A second attempt to colonize Vinland never got off the ground. When the Vikings landed, the Indians attacked them and drove them back to their ships. This ended the Vikings' hope of establishing further settlements in the New World. One more Viking ship did touch ground in Vinland in 1347, but its crew was only searching for wood. After the crew completed its task, the ship departed.

But what about the Minnesota Vikings of the National Football League? Doesn't their team name prove that the Norsemen pushed as far inland as Minnesota? Maybe and maybe not. A stone found on a farm near Kensington, Minnesota, contains writing that supposedly verifies a Viking visit in 1362. Although some authorities say the stone is authentic, others maintain it is a hoax. What do you think?

A statue of the great Viking leader Leif Ericson. What personal qualities does the statue seem to convey?

Name _____ Date _____

Name Those Explorers

Fill in the blank before each statement with a name from the word box. Several names are used more than once.

Alexander the Great

Eric the Red

General Hanno

Herodotus

Hippalus

Leif Ericson

Minoans

Phoenicians

Romans

Vikings

1. _____ Their civilization was centered on the island of Crete.

2. _____ They founded Carthage in north Africa.

3. _____ He is called the "Father of History."

4. _____ His expedition was attacked by screaming gorillas.

5. _____ He proved that the Black and Caspian seas are enclosed bodies of water.

6. _____ His empire extended all the way from Macedonia to India.

7. _____ He discovered that the monsoon winds blow in opposite directions at different times of the year.

8. _____ They discovered Cochin China.

9. _____ He gave Greenland its name.

10. _____ They came from the Scandinavian countries of Norway, Sweden, and Denmark.

11. _____ He called the area he explored Vinland.

12. _____ He was the first explorer to come ashore on land that later became the United States.

13. _____ Of all ancient peoples, they were the least interested in exploration.

From *Everyday Life: Exploration and Discovery* © 2005 Good Year Books.

Name _____ Date _____

Use Your Critical Thinking Skills

Think about the questions presented on this page. Then write your best answer to each on the lines provided.

1. People long ago believed that there were regions in the world where strange creatures existed. You have seen how General Hanno thought the gorillas that attacked his expedition were a race of huge savages. Other beliefs ranged from headless people whose faces were on their chests to men whose feet were so large they could lay on their backs and use their feet as umbrellas!

   One can easily see how General Hanno might mistake a gorilla for some kind of savage human. But what about headless people or those with umbrella-like feet? Or any race of creatures that were half beast and half man? How do you think such fanciful tales originated? On the lines below, give your opinions about the basis of such beliefs.

   _____

   _____

   _____

   _____

   _____

2. Leif Ericson came to America almost 500 years before Columbus. Why do you think he is not given credit for discovering the New World?

   _____

   _____

   _____

3. In your opinion, should Alexander the Great, who conquered almost all of the known world at the time, be included in a study of exploration? Why or why not?

   _____

   _____

   _____

Name _____ Date _____

Draw a Picture

In the space provided, draw and color a picture of a Viking ship. You can find examples in an encyclopedia, a history book, or on the Internet. On the lines at the bottom, write several facts about the ship you have sketched.

_____
_____
_____
_____
_____

From Everyday Life: Exploration and Discovery © 2005 GoodYear Books.

Name _____   Date _____

Brush Up on Your Geography

Reference was made in chapter 1 to many places touched by early explorers. How familiar are you with their locations and capitals? After consulting an atlas, dictionary, or encyclopedia, use the names in the word box below to answer the questions on the page.

Baghdad
Beirut
Canada
Canea
Colombo
Damascus
Godthaab
Greece
Hanoi
Iraq
Middle East
Persia
Sri Lanka
St. Johns
Teheran

1. The island of Crete is a part of the nation of _____. Crete's capital is _____.

2. You learned that Phoenicia was located approximately where Lebanon and Syria are today. Both Lebanon and Syria are countries in the _____. The capital of Lebanon is _____, while Syria's capital is _____.

3. Most of what was once Mesopotamia is today part of _____, the capital of which is _____.

4. Iran was once known as _____. Its capital is _____.

5. What was for centuries known as Ceylon is today called _____. Its capital is _____.

6. You learned that Cochin China was located where part of Vietnam is today. Once divided into North and South Vietnam, the country now is unified under a communist government. Its capital is _____.

7. The capital of Greenland is _____.

8. Newfoundland is a part of _____. Its capital is _____.

The Travels of Marco Polo

Skeptics called him one of Europe's greatest liars. Black stones (coal) that burned with a hot flame and provided heat for warmth and cooking? Fools who actually accepted paper money as payment instead of hard, precious metal? And a postal system that was well organized and efficient? "Come on, Marco," they must have said. "Surely you jest!"

But Marco Polo was not jesting. He had recently returned from a 20-year stay in Cathay (China) and saw firsthand the wonders he described to the doubting people of Venice, his hometown. Yet, no one believed him. Venetians, in fact, began to refer to any fanciful tale as a "Marco Polo." Even years later when he was on his deathbed, friends and family urged him to confess that he made up many of the stories told in his book, *The Book of Marco Polo* (or as some sources say, *Book of Marvels*). Many years passed before they and other Europeans came to realize that much of what Marco Polo was telling was the truth. (However, as we will soon see, some of what he described still seemed far-fetched.)

The Polos depart Venice in 1271 for China.

Marco's adventures in China stemmed from an earlier trip taken there by his father Nicolo and his uncle Maffeo. The Polo brothers were merchants who had traveled to China and won the favor of Kublai Khan, the Chinese emperor. After a stay of several years, Kublai Khan urged the Polo brothers to return to Venice and ask Pope Clement IV to send 100 Christians to China to instruct his people in the arts and ways of Europe. Before the Polos could embark on a second trip, however, Clement IV died, and the new pope, Gregory X, never warmed to the idea. Gregory sent only two friars (monks) to accompany the merchant brothers, and both of them turned back early in the trip.

When Nicolo and Maffeo Polo departed Venice in 1271, they took Nicolo's 17-year-old son, Marco, with them. Marco was delighted. "My cup of joy was full," he wrote later. He completed that statement by saying his one desire was to see the world. Can you imagine how excited a young boy of 17 was at the thought of such an adventure?

From *Everyday Life: Exploration and Discovery* © 2005 Good Year Books.

Little did the three Polos realize that the trip would take more than three years. After crossing Armenia in Turkey, Marco fell ill in Persia. It took a full year for him to recover. While he was recuperating in the mountains, his father and uncle traded and did business in the surrounding towns.

When young Marco regained his health, the trio crossed high mountains into the great Gobi Desert. The Gobi lies mainly in Mongolia and encompasses (covers) some 500,000 square miles of sand and wasteland. It took the Polos 30 days to cross this vast expanse, and Marco was happy to see the Khan's messengers waiting at its borders to guide them the rest of the way. They finally arrived at the court of the Great Khan in May of 1275.

Kublai Khan greeted the Polos with great friendship. Upon noticing Marco, the Khan asked Nicolo who this magnificent lad was. Nicolo replied, "He is my son and your servant." This response pleased the Great Khan, and he took an immediate liking to Marco. In a short time he began to confide in the intelligent young Venetian and to seek his advice on important matters. After several years he even appointed Marco to a high government post.

Although no more than 21 years old, Marco Polo became governor of the city of Yang Chow. He served in this position for three years, during which time he was afforded the opportunity to travel throughout Kublai Khan's vast realm. He also made trips to Tibet, Burma (Myanmar), Siam (Thailand), Ceylon (Sri Lanka), and India. He later described everything he saw in his book.

Marco Polo was astounded at the size and layout of China's cities. He was also struck by their cleanliness. Streets were paved and there were many bathhouses. (Remember that at that time in Europe, people seldom bathed.) One city in the south of China, Marco claimed, had 4,000 public baths. In addition, Chinese cities were safer than those in Europe. Firemen kept fires under control and policemen maintained law and order.

The palace of Kublai Khan in Peking (now Beijing) was another wonder of which Marco Polo later wrote. He described its reception room as so large that it could accommodate 5,000 people at one time. However, this is one example of a story that made people question Marco's credibility. Even some authors who have written on the China of that time seem to have allowed themselves considerable freedom in sorting through Marco Polo's assertions. One author refers to Kublai Khan's palace as lying within the famous "Forbidden City," the sequestered "city" within the city of Peking where the emperor lived and held court. A quick check of the historical record, however, shows that construction on the Forbidden City did not begin until 1420. By that date, Kublai Khan

had been dead 126 years and Marco Polo almost 100. This and other inconsistencies taint the story of Marco Polo.

Marco Polo was fairly accurate, however, in his description of the city of Peking. He writes that the city was built in the form of a square measuring six miles on each side. It was surrounded by an earthen wall some 50 feet high and had 12 gates. Its streets were so wide and so straight that no gate could be seen from another. It contained many magnificent houses and palaces. The only questionable point about Marco's description of Peking is his statement that each of the 12 gates were manned by 1,000 soldiers. Did he mean 1,000 at one time, or did the 1,000 rotate in shifts? It hardly seems likely that 1,000 men could be on duty at one gate at the same time.

Even more difficult to believe is how Marco Polo described the southern Chinese city of Hang-tcheou-fou. He asserts that the city measured 100 miles in circumference and had 12,000 stone bridges. One hundred miles in circumference and 12,000 bridges seems exaggerated. Furthermore, Marco stated that Kublai Khan's southern palace was so large that he could entertain 40,000 guests at one time. Forty thousand guests at one time? He also stated that on one occasion the emperor received as gifts 5,000 camels, 100,000 horses, and 5,000 elephants covered with cloth of gold and silver. Maybe he did—who knows? But do you believe Marco's story about a large, unchained lion being led to the Great Khan's throne and the beast kneeling before him in a show of humility and submission?

The Mongol ruler Kublai Khan, who, as emperor of China, confided in young Marco Polo and appointed him to an important government position.

At this point you must be wondering if anything Marco Polo said can be taken seriously. Rest assured that most of what he related about China was factual. As previously mentioned, the Chinese did use paper money, heat their homes with coal, and benefit from clean streets and the services of able firemen and policemen. They also were served by an efficient postal system, one that could boast of some 10,000 post offices spaced 25 miles apart and serviced by thousands of horses and riders. These and other tales told by Marco Polo are certainly true.

From *Everyday Life: Exploration and Discovery* © 2005 Good Year Books.

The Polos' long stay in China was not of their own choosing. Kublai Khan valued their services so much that he refused to let them leave. Finally, an opportunity arose that afforded them the break they sought. A beautiful Chinese princess had been betrothed to Kublai Kahn's great-nephew, who was a Persian prince, and, with travel anywhere at that time extremely dangerous, the Polos volunteered to escort her to her new home. The Great Khan accepted their offer, assuming they would return to China after their mission was completed.

Traveling by water around China and India, the Polos dropped off the princess in Persia and never looked back. In 1295 they arrived in Venice, where they were met with some suspicion by their fellow Venetians. After all, they had been away for 20 years, and they suddenly showed up relating tales that were difficult to believe. Their clothes were also tattered and they had almost forgotten how to speak Italian. They seemed like total strangers to the hometown folk.

In 1296, soon after arriving home, Marco became involved in a war between Venice and Genoa. He volunteered to command a Venetian ship, which resulted in his capture. He spent three years in a Genoese prison, and it was while in prison that he dictated his famous book to a fellow inmate.

Although much of what Marco Polo wrote about is open to question, his book enthralled readers and intensified interest in the Orient. His descriptions of the routes he took to and from China enabled mapmakers to draw more accurate maps that proved invaluable to later explorers. As much as anything else, the travels of Marco Polo helped bring on the Age of Exploration and Discovery that began in Europe in the 1400s.

A hunting party of the Great Khan. Displays such as these must have awed Marco Polo and his father and uncle.

Name _____ Date _____

Draw a Map

In the space below, draw a map depicting the routes followed by Marco Polo to and from China. Use a solid line to indicate one route and a broken line to illustrate the other. Be sure your map includes all of the world from Italy eastward to China.

You can find examples of maps of Marco Polo's travels in an encyclopedia or a history textbook.

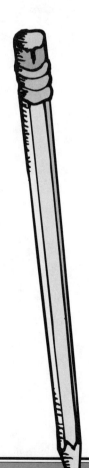

From *Everyday Life: Exploration and Discovery* © 2005 Good Year Books.

Name _____ Date _____

Create a Diary Entry

Marco Polo, his father, and his uncle saw wonders in China that Europeans at the time could not imagine. One of these wonders was fireworks.

Some records show that the Chinese were using firecrackers as early as the 600s. By the time the Polos arrived, the Chinese had surely become experts at illuminating the night sky with a variety of explosives. You can imagine how amazed the Polos were the first time they were treated to such an event.

On the lines provided, create a diary entry for June 15, 1275, in which Marco records his thoughts about the wonders of fireworks.

From Everyday Life: Exploration and Discovery © 2005 Good Year Books.

Name _____ Date _____

Make False Statements True

All of the statements on this page are false. Change the word(s) in *italics* to make them true. Write the replacement word(s) on the lines following the statements.

1. In Marco Polo's time, China was known as *Siam*.
   _____

2. Marco Polo was from the Italian city of *Genoa*.
   _____

3. Maffeo Polo was Marco Polo's *father*.
   _____

4. Marco Polo was *15* years old when he accompanied his father and uncle to China. _____

5. The Polos' trip to China took *six* years.
   _____

6. While en route to China, Marco Polo became ill when the party reached *Tibet*. _____

7. The Gobi Desert lies mainly in *India*.
   _____

8. *Thailand* today is know as Sri Lanka. _____

9. *Cipango* is the modern name for Burma.
   _____

10. Beijing, the capital of modern China, was known in Marco Polo's as time as *Yang Chow*. _____

11. Marco Polo was surprised to learn that the Chinese transacted business using *gold coins*. _____

12. When the Polos finally left China, they escorted a young Chinese princess who had been betrothed to a prince in *India*. _____

13. Marco Polo became a prisoner in 1296 as a result of a war between Venice and *Florence*. _____

From Everyday Life: Exploration and Discovery © 2005 Good Year Books.

Name _____   Date _____

Name Those Synonyms and Antonyms

A synonym is a word that has the same meaning as another word. An antonym is a word with a meaning that is the opposite of another word.

Below is a list of 20 words taken from the chapter. Write a synonym and an antonym for each. You may use a thesaurus or dictionary, if necessary.

		Synonym	**Antonym**
1.	efficient (adj)	_____	_____
2.	urge (v)	_____	_____
3.	far-fetched (adj)	_____	_____
4.	departed (v)	_____	_____
5.	delighted (adj)	_____	_____
6.	magnificent (adj)	_____	_____
7.	seldom (adv)	_____	_____
8.	accurate (adj)	_____	_____
9.	straight (adj)	_____	_____
10.	difficult (adj)	_____	_____
11.	benefit (n)	_____	_____
12.	able (adj)	_____	_____
13.	accepted (v)	_____	_____
14.	precious (adj)	_____	_____
15.	accompany (v)	_____	_____
16.	full (adj)	_____	_____
17.	completed (v)	_____	_____
18.	vast (adj)	_____	_____
19.	pleased (v)	_____	_____
20.	humility (n)	_____	_____

CHAPTER 3

The Terrible Sea of Darkness

The date was August 3, 1492. The place was Palos, Spain. Christopher Columbus, with three small ships and a total crew of less than 100 men, was about to embark on a great adventure—an adventure that would take him across the Atlantic Ocean to discover a New World.

During the Middle Ages, Europeans held strange beliefs about Africa and Asia. Such beliefs included the mythical creatures depicted in this drawing.

Christopher Columbus was an intelligent man who was convinced that the world was round. Never for a moment did he think his ships would sail out and fall off the face of Earth. However, the common sailor had little education and still clung to the medieval belief that the world was a flat disk surrounded by water. If one sailed out far enough, the seaman reasoned, his ship was bound to fall into oblivion. That is why for centuries sailors had hugged the coasts and never ventured out of sight of land.

What worried sailors of the time even more than the prospect of falling into a bottomless abyss was being done in by some kind of sea monster. So great was this fear that the part of the Atlantic Ocean that was beyond any known land was referred to as the "Sea of Darkness." One can imagine the anxiety felt by the wives and loved ones of Columbus's crews as the three ships sailed out of sight that August day in 1492. Would they fall off the face of Earth? Would the ships be smashed to pieces by terrible storms or even more terrible sea monsters? Would gigantic sea serpents snatch screaming sailors from the decks of their ships and devour them? Would these worried women ever see their sailor husbands, sweethearts, or sons again?

It seems only natural that medieval people would assume that monsters inhabited the seas. They had, after all, believed for centuries that mythical creatures roamed the land areas of Africa and Asia. Remember the headless race

From *Everyday Life: Exploration and Discovery* © 2005 Good Year Books.

whose faces were in their chests and the men whose feet were so large they could be used as umbrellas when their owners were lying down? Parts of Africa and Asia were said to contain treasures that were guarded by dragons and large, legless birds, the latter of whom lived their entire lives in the air. There were also sheep as large as oxen and women with eyes of brilliant jewels whose glare could slay a man in a moment. Moreover, there was supposed to be a river of gold that any person who entered could never escape alive.

A woodcut of an old map showing sea monsters sailors believed roamed the seas.

But on to sea monsters. Sea monsters were believed to come in all shapes and sizes. Some resembled huge snakes; others looked like dragons or gigantic fish. One sketch of the 1400s showed a creature that looked like a bloated toad, except that it had 12 legs. Other drawings depict monsters different in appearance from any animal known at the time. Regardless of shape or the number of appendages or fins, sailors placed the lengths of various sea monsters at from 25 to 100 feet. Some had snakelike heads; others had heads resembling dinosaurs or giraffes. All seemed to have fiery eyes that personified evil. Colors ranged from black to amber to dark brown.

Certain mythical creatures had "been around" for centuries. You might have heard of the Hydra. It was believed to be a serpent monster with nine heads. Each time an attacker chopped off one head, two grew in its place. (Wouldn't that be frustrating for a want-to-be hero?) Superhero Hercules of Greek mythology, however, successfully did in the Hydra with the help of his nephew, Iolaus. Each time Hercules lopped off a head, Iolaus hurried to cauterize or burn the roots, thus preventing new heads from sprouting. Medieval sailors who had heard of the Hydra, might have wondered if there were other Hydras lurking somewhere in the Sea of Darkness. Or something worse?

In addition to fire-breathing, dragonlike sea serpents, medieval seaman feared ocean monsters whose massive jaws and powerful tails could smash a ship to smithereens. There were also believed to be gigantic fish capable of creating whirlpools that could send a ship to the bottom and huge hands that

might reach up and pull a ship under. As late as the 1500s, when the Protestant Revolt was in full swing and respect for the Roman Catholic Church had dwindled in some countries, there was even a sea monster described as resembling a bishop in religious garb! How's that for imagination?

The kraken, the most feared of mythical sea monsters. In reality, it was probably a giant squid, but it is doubtful if it was large enough to sink a ship.

No sea monster, however, was more feared than the terrible kraken. Sketches made of this creature depict it as either a colossal octopus or a giant squid. In all probability, it was the latter. It was said to be so large and its tentacles so long that it could reach to the top of a ship and pull it under, drowning its crew. Imagine the fear in a seaman's eyes as he listened to tales of such a monster!

Fact or fiction? You might be surprised to learn that giant squids do exist and that there is some evidence of their having "attacked" ships in the past. Even ships in modern times have had encounters with these creatures. The logs of a number of vessels report such incidents, but, each ship's screw propeller made sure the squids always got the worst of any encounter. Whether the squids in question actually attacked the ships or simply bumped into them is open to conjecture. One thing, however, is certain: If the giant squid of old actually existed, it would have had no trouble reaching out of the water and capsizing a ship. Ships at the time of Columbus were less than 100 feet in length; the giant squid was said to measure 100 feet across its body and to weigh 10 tons. What do you think?

If sailors of old managed to elude all the sea monsters bent on doing them in, there were always the many dangers of the ocean itself. Treacherous storms created huge waves capable of sinking most ships. There was the dreaded equator, where the water was so hot that it might burn a ship to a crisp. If, by some chance, a ship escaped a fiery death, the danger was far from over. The water around the equator was thought to be as thick as molasses; once a ship entered, it could never leave.

From *Everyday Life: Exploration and Discovery* © 2005 Good Year Books.

There is more. Medieval people believed that the islands near the equator were inhabited by demons. Furthermore, these islands often floated away upon being approached. The only human inhabitants of this eerie world were lost souls doomed to spend eternity wandering about with no hope of ever escaping. With such commonly held beliefs, it is easy to see why for centuries sailors avoided the Sea of Darkness.

So, you might ask, are any of the old myths and superstitions about the ocean believable? Except for the giant squid, it is probably safe to say that none of the adverse oceanic conditions and terrible monsters feared by early sailors ever existed. The equator is not the horrible place it was once thought to be, and reports of sea monsters have been debunked as being nothing more than whales, logs, trees, canoes, parts of wrecked ships, and gobs of seaweed.

But, some people might say, can we be sure? They can cite the case of the coelacanth to make their point. The coelacanth is a giant fish that was once thought to have been extinct for more than 65 million years. Then one was caught off the tip of South Africa in 1938. If the coelacanth still exists, is it possible that other creatures that modern sailors have never seen also exist?

A coelacanth.

Name _____ Date _____

Finish a Story

In chapter 3 you learned about the fears sailors once had of crossing the oceans. Not the least of these fears had to do with sea monsters. With this in mind, complete a story that has been started for you. Lines are provided for you to expand on the story and to give it any ending you desire. Use the back of the page, if necessary. On a separate piece of paper, illustrate the sea monster that Carlos and Francisco saw.

Carlos and Francisco were standing on deck enjoying the tranquility of the ocean. The storm had passed, the weather was clear, and all seemed right with the world.

Suddenly, Francisco pointed to something in the water off the starboard side.

"Carlos! Look! What in heaven's name is that?" the startled seaman exclaimed.

"I'm not sure," answered Carlos, equally alarmed. "Whatever it is is heading straight for the ship. Look! I think it's some kind of a sea serpent. Oh, man! Look at the size of that thing!"

_____

_____

_____

_____

_____

_____

_____

_____

_____

_____

_____

_____

_____

From Everyday Life: Exploration and Discovery © 2005 Good Year Books.

Name _____ Date _____

Participate in a Skit

Divide the class into groups and have each choose one of the skits. Students should use their imagination and creative skills in planning their skit, which should be about five minutes in length.

Students not participating directly in a skit can make simple props and costumes or critique and rate the skits at the conclusion of the activity.

There is a lead-in to each skit to help students in their planning.

Skit 1—A Sea Captain Trying to Recruit Sailors for a Voyage

Early sea captains sometimes had trouble getting men to sign on for voyages into the unknown. Maps were still primitive, ships were small and often unseaworthy, and untold dangers—whether real or imagined—awaited sailors who ventured out of sight of land.

Create this skit around a sea captain trying to round up sailors for a voyage into the Sea of Darkness.

Skit 2—A Husband and Father Taking Leave of His Family

Imagine the heart-rending scene of a sailor in the 1400s bidding his wife and children farewell before boarding a ship for a faraway journey into uncharted waters.

Center this skit around the dialogue that probably took place at the time.

Skit 3—A Boy Contemplating a Career at Sea

Sometimes youngsters who were not yet 10 years old went to sea and served as cabin boys on ships. Create a skit focusing on a young lad discussing with his friends the possibility of running away and embarking on such an adventure.

Skit 4—A Sailor Relating Tales of the Kraken

In chapter 3 you read about the kraken, the gigantic, mythical, squidlike creature so feared by early seaman. Create a skit in which several sailors share "tales" of encounters with this terrible monster.

Name _____ Date _____

Do Research on Scurvy

Treacherous seas and the fear of confronting terrible monsters were not the only perils associated with long sea voyages. Another was scurvy, a dread disease that took the lives of many seamen before it was fully understood and conquered.

Look up *scurvy* in an encyclopedia or some other source and answer the questions below.

1. What is scurvy and what causes it?

_____
_____
_____
_____

2. What are the symptoms of scurvy?

_____
_____
_____
_____

3. Why were sailors in the past so susceptible to scurvy?

_____
_____
_____

4. How is scurvy prevented and treated?

_____
_____
_____

5. Can you deduce from your research why British sailors came to be called *limeys*?

_____
_____
_____

From Everyday Life: Exploration and Discovery © 2005 Good Year Books.

Name _____ Date _____

Distinguish between Sentences and Fragments

Can you tell when a statement is a complete sentence and not just a fragment? Fragments are statements that lack either a verb or a subject or do not express a complete thought. Authors sometimes use fragments in certain situations, but, as a student, you should always use complete sentences when writing.

Below are nine statements. Some are fragments, while others are complete sentences. On the line to the left of each, write F if the statement is a fragment or S if it is a complete sentence. Lines are provided for you to make complete sentences of those statements you mark as fragments.

1. _____ The Sea of Darkness, feared by all early seamen.

_____

2. _____ The kraken, believed to resemble a large squid, was thought to weigh 10 tons.

_____

3. _____ While the small ship almost capsized in the storm.

_____

4. _____ The Sea of Darkness was a name given to the Atlantic Ocean.

_____

5. _____ Although the Hydra was a mythical animal.

_____

6. _____ After a ceolacanth was caught in 1938.

_____

7. _____ People once believed the world was a flat disk.

_____

8. _____ No sooner had the serpent appeared.

_____

9. _____ Medieval sailors feared to sail in the waters near the equator.

_____

From Everyday Life: Exploration and Discovery © 2005 Good Year Books.

The Lure of the East

People may have laughed at Marco Polo and referred to his tales of adventure as "Marco Polos." Or they might have called him "Marco Millions" because he constantly raved about the millions of people who lived in Cathay's cities and the millions in wealth possessed by Kublai Khan. But they didn't laugh when they saw the jewels that Marco Polo, his father, and his uncle brought back to Venice stitched into their clothing. Maybe Marco stretched the truth a bit when he talked about all the other wonders he had seen, but he certainly didn't lie about the rubies, emeralds, and other precious gems. And when his book came out later and circulated throughout Europe, it created an even greater interest in the East and its prized goods and riches.

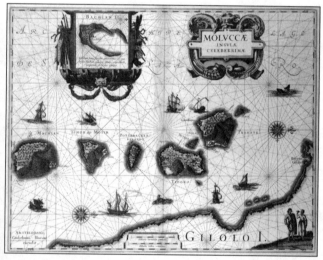

The desire for spices led Europeans to seek an all-water route to the Molucca, or Spice, Islands in the fifteenth century. The Moluccas appear near the top of the map.

Before proceeding, it would be helpful to point out what was meant at the time by the "East" or, more accurately, the "East Indies." Today the East Indies, in its narrowest sense, refers to the area known as the Malay Archipelago. (An archipelago is a group of many islands.) It lies southeast of Asia and includes the Philippines, Sumatra, Borneo, Timor, Celebes, and the Moluccas. In short, the East Indies today, except for the Philippines, can be roughly equated to the nation of Indonesia.

At the beginning of the Age of Exploration in the 1400s, the East Indies was the name applied collectively to Cathay (China), Cipango (Japan), India, and Indonesia. Although the Polos' display of valuable gems from China dazzled the residents of Venice, it was on Indonesia, and particularly on the Molucca Islands, that the attention of European governments and explorers was focused. This was due to the spices indigenous, or native, to these islands. Because pepper, cloves, cinnamon, nutmeg, and other spices were found there in abundance, early mapmakers and seamen referred to the Moluccas as the "Spice Islands." It was these islands that Columbus hoped to reach when he set sail in 1492.

The desire for spices, therefore, was a leading factor that helped bring on the Age of Exploration and Discovery. Spices not only made food taste better but rendered spoiled foods, especially meats, edible. With refrigeration

From *Everyday Life: Exploration and Discovery* © 2005 Good Year Books.

centuries into the future and meats often having to travel long distances before they reached the buyer's table, the need for spices was a priority with Europeans.

The people of Europe had become familiar with spices and other products of the East as a result of the Crusades. From 1096 to about 1291, with periods of peace in between, Christian Crusaders had fought to regain the Holy Land (Palestine) from the Muslim Turks. They never succeeded, but in the process they were introduced to goods seldom seen in Europe. In addition to spices, Crusaders were amazed at the variety of silks, glassware, gems, dyes, perfumes, and rugs they saw for the first time. As a result, a lively trade developed between the West and the East.

Although Europeans enjoyed the flow of Eastern goods into their countries, they did not relish the prices they had to pay for them. Trade between western Europe and the East was monopolized by the Italian city-states of Genoa, Pisa, and Venice. Located on the Mediterranean and Adriatic seas and therefore within easy sailing distance to Constantinople and other places where trade caravans arrived, merchant ships of these cities picked up Eastern goods and brought them to Europe. There they charged exorbitant (very high) prices for everything they sold. One can't completely blame the Italians, though. By the time goods traveled overland from Asia to Constantinople or Alexandria in Egypt, they passed through many hands. Each time, the price went up. This was especially true of spices. When these much-coveted food enhancers and preservers finally reached the tables of Europe, they cost 20 times more than the original cost in the East.

The desire of European nations to bypass the Italian monopoly and seek an all-water route to the East was another factor that brought on the Age of Exploration. Then, in 1453, Constantinople, the capital of the Byzantine or Eastern Roman Empire, fell to the Turks. This made a new route to the East even more imperative. The Turks imposed heavy tolls on Europeans traders and often attacked European merchant ships in the Mediterranean. Faced with this additional obstacle, the rulers of Europe began to finance expeditions in search of new trade routes.

The need of European governments for metal for making coins was another reason for exploration. Gold deposits had almost been used up, and the silver mines of what later became Germany could not meet the demand for their product. With metal coins needed for business transactions and trade, a new source of gold and silver had to be found. The monarchies of Europe looked East for this source.

Still another reason for exploration was the desire to spread Christianity among the "heathen" peoples of the world. These included all the inhabitants of China, Japan, Africa, the East Indies, and elsewhere. Europeans, in fact, came to believe that it was their duty to convert such non-believers to the Christian faith. Besides, they reasoned, the spreading of Christianity had a practical side. Converted natives and their rulers were easier to control and were therefore not likely to cause problems.

To a certain degree, the Renaissance produced yet another reason for exploration: a thirst for knowledge about foreign lands. During a large part of the Middle Ages, most Europeans could have cared less about what was going on in the rest of the world. Their existence focused on scratching out a living, and many, such as the serfs on the manors, lived their entire lives without venturing five miles in any direction. But with the appearance of stable governments and the end of feudalism, people grew interested in other things. They not only wondered what lay just beyond the next hill but what it was like across the river, the sea, or the ocean. Although not a major factor in bringing on the Age of Exploration and Discovery, the desire for knowledge did play a minor role.

The necessity of finding new sources of gold from which to mint coins was one factor that brought on the Age of Exploration and Discovery.

Finally, the prospect of adventure attracted many to exploration. Just as the thrill of adventure lured some settlers to early America and pioneers to the great American West (and astronauts to outer space many years later), so too did it beckon the seaman of the 1400s. Certainly a long sea voyage was frightening and fraught with danger, but life at home wasn't exactly a bed of roses either. While a sailor's chance of surviving a trip across the Atlantic was 50–50 at best, his likelihood of living beyond the age of 30 if he stayed home on the farm might be even less. Yes, he might die of scurvy or malnutrition at sea, or he might go down with his ship in a storm. Some terrible sea monster might even devour him (or so many sailors believed). But if he remained in his native village, he was just as likely to die of the plague or some other mysterious illness. Given the choice, many able-bodied men chose to go to sea.

As for the commanders of the various expeditions, they were driven by the hope of honor and glory. Few explorers grew rich from their exploits. Only

From *Everyday Life: Exploration and Discovery* © 2005 Good Year Books.

conquistadors such as Francisco Pizarro and Hernando Cortés became wealthy men at the expense of the Indians of Latin America. Even Columbus, who made four trips across the Atlantic, died a poor man. Most of the wealth discovered in the New World was shipped back to the various crowns of Europe.

All the motives in the world could not have brought on the Age of Exploration and Discovery alone. There also had to be improved ships and instruments to make long voyages possible. By the latter part of the 1400s, ships were being built that could better withstand the rigors of ocean travel. They were full-rigged ships, which meant they had both square and lateen sails. The latter type of sail is triangular in shape, making it possible for a ship to sail into the wind. Such ships were also improved and made faster when shipbuilders began placing the steering rudder at the stern (rear) of a vessel instead of on the side.

Two navigational instruments made long voyages possible. One was the compass, which was invented by the Chinese and passed on by the Arabs. The compass, of course, enabled seamen to always locate north and therefore know in which direction they were sailing. Another instrument was the astrolabe. With this device, sailors could find their positions at sea by determining a ship's latitude.

By the latter part of the 1400s, European nations had the motives and the means to launch the Age of Exploration and Discovery. All that remained was for someone to provide the inspiration and the impetus. That someone was Prince Henry of Portugal.

The astrolabe, a navigational device that helped seamen determine latitude and thus the location of their ship at sea.

Name _____ Date _____

Fill in a Map of the East Indies

Ⓞn the map below that corresponds roughly to the East Indies today, fill in the places at right:

Color your map for effect.

Borneo	Java	New Guinea
Brunei	Java Sea	Sumatra
Celebes	Malaysia	Timor
Celebes Sea	Moluccas	Timor Sea

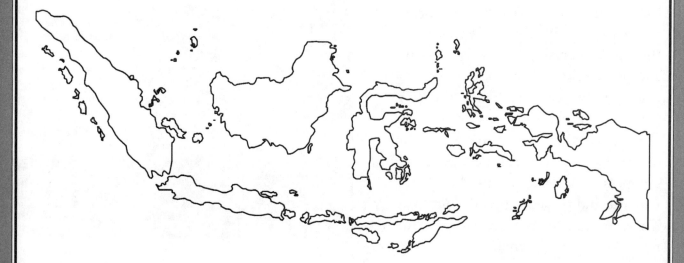

From Everyday Life: Exploration and Discovery © 2005 Good Year Books.

Name _____ *Date* _____

Identify Those Spices

Listed below are 20 common spices used in everyday cooking. You have probably noticed most of them either at home or in the spice section of your local food market.

On the line to the right of each spice, write one way in which it is used in cooking (for example, "on pizza," "in stews," etc.). Consult a cookbook or an encyclopedia, or ask your parent or guardian for help. Then choose one spice to bring in and show to the class.

1. allspice _____

2. anise _____

3. basil _____

4. bay leaves _____

5. chili powder _____

6. cinnamon _____

7. cloves _____

8. cumin _____

9. ginger _____

10. marjoram _____

11. mint _____

12. mustard _____

13. nutmeg _____

14. oregano _____

15. paprika _____

16. parsley _____

17. pepper _____

18. sage _____

19. sesame seed _____

20. thyme _____

From Everyday Life: Exploration and Discovery © 2005 Good Year Books.

Name _____ Date _____

Fill in a Venn Diagram

You probably never thought of it before, but there are similarities between the Exploration of Space today and the Age of Exploration and Discovery more than 500 years ago. With this thought in mind, put on your thinking cap and fill in the Venn diagram with facts about the two periods. In the area where the circles overlap, list features common to both.

Age of Exploration

Both

Exploration of Space

From Everyday Life: Exploration and Discovery © 2005 Good Year Books.

Name _____ Date _____

Complete a Vocabulary Exercise

Select the meaning of each word as it is used in chapter 4. Write the letter of the correct meaning on the line at the left. The paragraph in which each word appears in the narrative is written in parentheses.

_____ 1. possessed (paragraph 1)

(a) owned
(b) influenced strongly
(c) controlled by an evil spirit

_____ 2. precious (paragraph 1)

(a) too nice
(b) much loved
(c) valuable

_____ 3. bypass (paragraph 7)

(a) go over the head of someone to a higher authority
(b) avoid
(c) a road around a city

_____ 4. capital (paragraph 7)

(a) city where the seat of a government is located
(b) amount of money
(c) main or most important

_____ 5. stable (paragraph 10)

(a) steadfast
(b) not likely to fall or be overthrown
(c) building in which horses or other animals are kept

_____ 6. minor (paragraph 10)

(a) under the legal age of responsibility
(b) course of study in college
(c) less important

_____ 7. plague (paragraph 11)

(a) a contagious disease
(b) bother
(c) punishment thought to be sent from God

CHAPTER 5

Portugal Leads the Way

His father was King John I of Portugal. He was handsome and muscular, with blonde hair inherited from his English mother, whom his father married after making an alliance with England in 1386. He was forward-thinking and wanted to see his country achieve greatness. He was Prince Henry, referred to in history as "the Navigator" because of his interest and support of seafaring adventures.

Prince Henry the Navigator had two important goals for Portugal. First, he wanted to find the source of the gold, ivory, slaves, and spices that Arab traders had monopolized for centuries. He correctly reasoned this source to be near the Gulf of Guinea on Africa's west coast. If his country could wrest control of this lucrative trade from the Muslims and establish trading posts in the region, it would become the richest and most powerful nation in Europe.

Henry's second goal was shrouded in mystery. He, like many others at the time, wanted to locate the legendary Prestor John. Prestor John was believed to be a Christian king who ruled over a vast area of Asia in the 1100s. He was thought to be a direct descendant of the Magi, the Three Wise Men said to have brought gifts to the baby Jesus. The belief in Prestor John was so strong that Pope Alexander III sent a messenger from Rome to look for him in 1177. The messenger never returned, but the belief in the mythical king persisted.

By Prince Henry's time, Prestor John would have been almost 300 years old! Europeans, however, still insisted he was real and continued efforts to find him. Prince Henry thought the Christian king ruled somewhere in Africa, possibly in what is now Ethiopia. He hoped to link up with Prestor John and organize a joint crusade to drive the Muslims from both North Africa and the Holy Land.

To realize his dreams, Prince Henry established a school for navigators at Sagres, on the Portuguese coast. Here gathered the leading sailors, mapmakers, astronomers, and shipbuilders of the day. Numbered among their ranks were Arabs and Italians, who knew more about the seas and navigation than anyone at the time. These learned instructors taught sailors cartography (mapmaking) and the use of such new instruments as the compass and the astrolabe. They also developed the caravel, a new and sturdier ship that sailed along at a faster speed because of its lateen, or triangular, sails.

Henry sent out expeditions that rediscovered and claimed for Portugal the Azores and the Madeiras in the Atlantic. His ships then turned south and

proceeded—year by year—to inch their way along the west coast of Africa. In 1441, a sea captain named Antao Goncalves brought home to Portugal the first cargo of gold and slaves. By this time, Henry had come to believe that India and other areas of the East could be reached by sailing around Africa. He died in 1460, however, before his assumption could be proven.

No one knew just how far to the south Africa extended. Portuguese ships had made their way along a 1,500-mile stretch of the coast and had still not reached the tip. To everyone anxious to reap the benefits of India's riches, it seemed that Africa went on forever.

It was not until 1486 that a sea captain named Bartholomeu Diaz (or Dias) proved Prince Henry right. Diaz actually sailed around Africa's southern tip and was on his way to the Indian Ocean, although he did not realize it at the time. But we are ahead of our story.

Bartholomeu Diaz left Lisbon in 1486 with three caravels. He was under orders from King John II to not only sail around Africa and chart the way to India but to find the elusive Prestor John as well. After hugging the coast for weeks and unknowingly getting close to his goal, Diaz's three ships met heavy winds, which blew them off course and away from land. For 13 days they drifted, and Diaz had no idea as to his location. When the winds finally subsided, his vessels had somehow been blown around the tip of Africa and were at the edge of the Indian Ocean. Diaz believed he had found the way to India, and he naturally wanted to go on. But his crews were weary of sailing through rough seas and demanded they turn around and return home. Faced with the likelihood of mutiny, Diaz had no choice but to bow to their wishes.

Prince Henry the Navigator. His interest in exploration led to the voyages of discovery that began in the fifteenth century.

On the way back to Portugal, Diaz's ships passed through what became known as the Cape of Good Hope. Because of the near-tragic consequences his ships almost faced there, Diaz called it the Cape of Storms. Upon being informed of Diaz's achievement, King John renamed it the Cape of Good Hope. The king believed that the cape was good for the future of Portugal.

Nine years passed before another Portuguese explorer followed Diaz's route and sailed on to India. This explorer was Vasco da Gama. In 1497, he was sent by King Manuel I to complete what Diaz had started. He left Lisbon in July of that year, with four ships and 200 men, one of whom was Bartholomeu Diaz.

Stamp depicting Vasco da Gama, the first European to sail around the Cape of Good Hope to India.

Taking Diaz's advice, da Gama did not hug the coast as his predecessor had done. Instead, he sailed far out into the Atlantic before turning south. By doing so, he avoided the stormy seas that Diaz had experienced. In November 1497, da Gama's expedition rounded the Cape of Good Hope after having sailed some 4,000 miles. It then sailed about halfway up the eastern coast of Africa before heading across the Indian Ocean toward India. The ships arrived intact at Calicut, India, on May 22, 1498.

Da Gama's voyage to and from India took 26 months and covered about 24,000 miles, approximately the circumference of Earth, making the expedition even more remarkable. Also, the two-year journey was fraught with danger, unfriendly and sometimes hostile Indian rulers and Arab traders, and disease. Of the 200 men who left Lisbon on July 8, 1497, only 60 returned in 1499. Some sources place this number even lower, at 44.

In spite of the hardships and great loss of life, the Portuguese Crown viewed da Gama's expedition as a great success. The few jewels, spices, and silks he brought back paid for the cost of the voyage some 60 times over. More importantly, the expedition opened an all-water route to the East, making Portugal for a short time the richest and most powerful country in Europe.

One year after the completion of da Gama's mission, the Portuguese discovered and claimed Brazil. This came about quite by accident. Pedro Alvarez Cabral was trying to follow da Gama's route to India when strong winds blew him off course. He ended up far westward in the Atlantic, and by the time he sighted land again he had reached Brazil. He claimed the huge area in the name of Portugal, even though the Spanish had arrived there first a short time earlier.

From *Everyday Life: Exploration and Discovery* © 2005 Good Year Books.

Cabral's return to Portugal with even more riches for the Crown was greeted with both excitement and sadness. The king was exuberant that another of his sea captains had claimed a vast area of the New World for his country. At the same time, he was despondent because the expedition had resulted in the death of a true Portuguese hero: Bartholomeu Diaz. Diaz, you will remember, had paved the way around the Cape of Good Hope 14 years earlier. Unfortunately for the famous discoverer and other crewmen, however, four of Cabral's ships sank on the return to Portugal, drowning all those aboard. Diaz was the captain of one of these ships.

Portugal was able to keep Brazil because of a treaty drawn up in 1493 by Pope Alexander VI. Because Portugal and Spain were competing for new discoveries, the pope drew an imaginary line that ran north and south through the Atlantic and just to the west of Brazil. Portugal had the right to all lands east of the line, which included Brazil and the East Indies. Spain was granted sole control over all area to the west of the line, which took in all of the Americas except Brazil. (No other European country had yet joined the race for colonies.)

As mentioned above, for a brief period Portugal reaped the benefits of its exploratory adventures. New and exotic products poured into the country, making it more prosperous than at any time in its history. The spices and other precious goods brought in from the East Indies made the Portuguese the envy of all Europe. Even though the route da Gama had taken to reach India was in time discovered by other countries, the Portuguese did their best to keep it a secret. Other nations knew of da Gama's accomplishment, but they had no idea how he had gotten there. They even resorted to using spies and bribery to learn the particulars of his voyage.

In chapter 6 you will read how Columbus's discovery of America led to Spain claiming and colonizing most of what is now Central and South America. Then, in chapter 7, you will read about the Spaniards' brutal treatment and exploitation of the Indians who inhabited those regions.

From Everyday Life: Exploration and Discovery © 2005 Good Year Books.

Name _____   Date _____

Solve Some Caravel Word Problems

In chapter 5 you learned that the Portuguese developed the caravel, the sailing ship that dominated the sea lanes at the beginning of the Age of Exploration and Discovery.

To the right are four word problems dealing with the caravel. Work each in the space provided and write the correct answer on the appropriate line.

1. A caravel was a very light ship. Ocean liners that later transported passengers across the oceans were extremely heavy, weighing as much as 50,000 tons. If the weight of an ocean liner was 1,000 times greater than that of a caravel, how much did a caravel weigh?

    _____ tons

2. A caravel might cover the 4,000-mile distance from Europe to the New World in about 33 days. With these figures in mind, answer the following questions:

    a. How many miles would a caravel average a day?

    _____ miles

    b. What speed (in mph) would it average?

    _____ mph

3. A ship's speed is actually measured in knots. One knot equals one nautical mile an hour. In round numbers, the nautical mile is 6,076 feet long. Thus a ship traveling at a speed of 15 knots can go 15 nautical miles an hour. How much longer is the nautical mile than the statute, or land, mile?

    _____ feet

From Everyday Life: Exploration and Discovery © 2005 Good Year Books.

Name _____ Date _____

Solve an Exploration Puzzle

ACROSS

2 Where Portuguese ships arrived in India

6 Shape of a caravel's sails

7 Ship developed by the Portuguese

9 Nationality of Prince Henry's mother

12 Portugal's rival for overseas possessions

13 First to sail to the tip of Africa

14 Prince Henry's country

DOWN

1 Prince Henry's father

3 Claimed Brazil for Portugal

4 _____ John

5 Site of Prince Henry's school

8 Prince _____

10 Cape of _____

11 First to sail around Africa to India

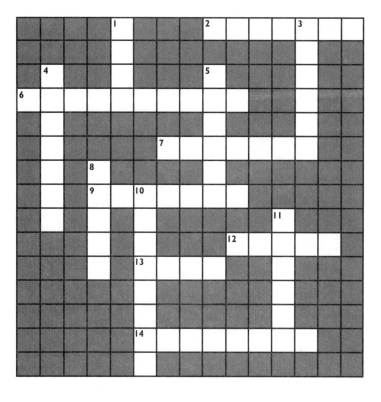

Name _____ Date _____

Interview Prince Henry

Imagine that newspapers were commonplace in the 1400s and that you are a reporter for the *Lisbon Daily Jabber*. Also imagine that you have been sent to Sagres to interview Prince Henry upon the opening of his school for navigators.

Write a report of your interview with the prince. Two questions you might ask the prince from the start are:

1. What caused you to become interested in exploration?

and

2. How do you think your school will benefit Portugal?

_____

_____

_____

_____

_____

_____

_____

_____

_____

_____

_____

_____

_____

_____

_____

_____

_____

_____

From Everyday Life: Exploration and Discovery © 2005 Good Year Books.

Name _____ Date _____

Do Research on Portugal

How much do you know about present-day Portugal? Can you point it out on a map? Do you know anything about its people or their means of livelihood?

Research Portugal in an up-to-date encyclopedia, almanac, or some other source. Then fill in the blanks to the questions at right.

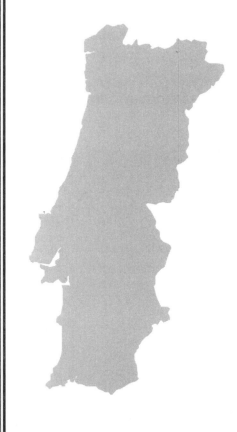

1. Portugal shares the _____ Peninsula with Spain.

2. The capital of Portugal is _____.

3. About 97% of all Portuguese belong to the _____ Church.

4. Portugal is bordered on the west by _____ _____.

5. In the late 1500s and early 1600s, Portugal was controlled by _____.

6. The approximate population of Portugal is _____.

7. Portugal's land area is _____ square miles.

8. Three important industries of Portugal are _____, _____, and _____.

9. The _____ is the monetary unit of Portugal.

10. The average life expectancy in Portugal is _____ years for men and _____ years for women.

11. Portugal has a _____ form of government.

12. Place the following events in Portugal's past history in chronological order by writing the numbers 1 to 5 in the blanks.

    _____ Da Gama sails around Africa to India.

    _____ Prince Henry establishes a school for navigators.

    _____ Cabral discovers and claims Brazil.

    _____ Prince Henry dies.

    _____ Diaz is the first to sail around the Cape of Good Hope.

Columbus Discovers a New World

During the years when the Portuguese were inching their way along the coast of Africa in the hope of finding an all-water route to the Indies, there lived in Portugal an Italian who had a different idea about how to get there. His name was Cristoforo Colombo, or Christopher Columbus as he is known in English. Columbus believed a ship could reach the Indies by sailing due west across the Ocean Sea, which is what the Atlantic Ocean was called in those days.

Christopher Columbus, who discovered the New World in 1492.

But wait a minute. Didn't most people believe Earth was flat and that by sailing west too far one would simply fall off its face? Well, the uneducated masses thought so, just as they believed in all manner of sea monsters. But men of knowledge and wisdom had known for centuries that the world was round. So, too, did Columbus, who, although he lacked formal schooling, had a good head on his shoulders. He had studied the maps of the ancient geographer Ptolemy and had read *The Book of Marco Polo*. All Columbus needed to prove his theories was for some European monarch to finance an expedition.

It was only natural that Columbus should first turn to King John II of Portugal. Since taking up residence there, he had sailed under the Portuguese flag on a number of occasions. He had also married Dona Felipa Perestrello, the daughter of the governor of one of the islands in the Portuguese-controlled Madeiras. Thus, by 1479, the year of his marriage, Columbus may have begun to think of himself as much Portuguese as Italian.

King John II was interested in Columbus's proposal. His court officials, however, advised caution. They reasoned that Columbus's estimation of the distance between the Canary Islands and Cipango (Japan) was off by a wide margin. After studying the maps of cartographer Paolo Toscanelli, Columbus had convinced himself that Cipango lay a scant 2,400 miles across the Atlantic. (The real distance from the Canaries to Japan, by airplane, is 10,600 miles.)

From *Everyday Life: Exploration and Discovery* © 2005 Good Year Books.

What neither Columbus nor Toscanelli, or anyone living in the 1400s, realized, however, was that the continents of North America and South America existed and stood in the way of any direct sea route to the East. King John and his advisers did not know this either, but they were certain that Cipango was much farther away than Columbus led them to believe. In addition, Columbus demanded much from the king in the way of titles and personal power. So, after listening to the plan presented to him in 1482, he turned down the discoverer of the New World.

Disappointed but undaunted, Columbus left for Spain in 1485 to present his proposal to King Ferdinand and Queen Isabella. A popular misconception of his audience with the monarchs is that he spent considerable time trying to convince them that Earth was round. Early textbooks, and possibly even some today, mention this. In reality, the matter of the shape of the earth never came up; discussion centered around the distance between Spain and Asia. As King John of Portugal did before them, Ferdinand and Isabella bowed to the wishes of their advisers and rejected Columbus's plea for ships and money.

Despite denying Columbus's proposal, King Ferdinand and Queen Isabella were keenly interested and showed their favor by putting him on the royal payroll. They postponed granting their approval because they were preoccupied at the time with driving the Moors (Muslims) from Granada, the last part of Spain not united under the Spanish crown. They had been waging war against the Moors for some time, and it was not until 1492 that they at last drove them out of Spain. Then and only then did they consider the proposal Columbus had presented to them.

By 1492, Columbus had given up hope of receiving backing from the Spanish king and queen. Having been turned down by the monarchs of both Spain and Portugal, he decided to board a ship for France and seek the backing of Charles VIII. Before he could leave, however, a messenger sent by Ferdinand and Isabella intercepted him and brought him back to the Spanish royal court.

This time the Spanish monarchs agreed to help Columbus. They gave him three ships and a crew of 88 men. The ships were the *Nina,* the *Pinta,* and the *Santa Maria.* The *Nina* and the *Pinta* were caravels, each approximately 70 feet long. The *Santa Maria* was a carrack, a larger vessel equipped with square sails. Ferdinand and Isabella also consented to Columbus's requests that he be made governor of all lands he discovered and that he receive 10 percent of all gold and other products he found. In addition, he was to receive the title "Admiral of the Ocean Sea."

From Everyday Life: Exploration and Discovery © 2005 Good Year Books.

On August 3, 1492, Columbus set sail from Palos, Spain. His destination was the Canary Islands, which lie some 60 miles off the northwest coast of Africa. He believed the Canaries to be located at the same latitude as Cipango and that by striking out due west from there, he could take advantage of the trade winds and cross the ocean in a month. The three ships under his command reached the islands in nine days, where they made necessary repairs and took on provisions.

A typical caravel. Two of Columbus's ships, the *Nina* and the *Pinta*, were caravels.

You are familiar with the story from here. Even with favorable winds and weather, the ships failed to sight land after a month. To prevent his anxious crews from growing even more restless, Columbus, as did many mariners at the time, kept two separate logs. One log was for his own use. The other he shared with his three crews. In the second log, he purposely minimized the distance covered for fear his men would mutiny. And, indeed, they would have had they known how far the three ships had actually sailed.

Sailors of the 1400s were a superstitious lot. Even when things were going well, they worried and fretted. The weather was good, they encountered no storms, and they had no lack of food to eat. Yet the fact that everything seemed perfect was a source of worry. With the skies so fair and blue, would it ever rain again? Would they all die of thirst so far from home? Would the winds be as favorable taking them home as they had been in bringing them so far west? Their minds seemed to constantly seek imagined horrors on which to dwell.

On October 10, after 30 days at sea and still no sight of land, the crew of the *Santa Maria* gave Columbus an ultimatum. If land was not sighted within two or three days, they would mutiny if he did not turn back for home. Luckily for the beleaguered (harassed) admiral, fate seemed to be on his side. At 2 A.M. on October 12, the lookout of the *Pinta* suddenly shouted "Land! Land!"

From *Everyday Life: Exploration and Discovery* © 2005 Good Year Books.

The land spotted from the *Pinta* was Watling Island in what is now the Bahamas. Columbus went ashore and named the island San Salvador, meaning "the Savior." He was met by friendly natives who told him about other nearby islands. Thinking he had reached the Indies, Columbus called the natives Indians. That is how Native Americans came to be known by that name.

Columbus stayed on Watling Island only a few days. He left to explore other islands in the area, still thinking he would find the mainland of Asia. But instead of the large cities, golden palaces, rich merchants, and bustling ports described by Marco Polo, he found only exotic birds and near-naked natives who painted their bodies. On this first trip to the New World, Columbus also discovered Cuba and Hispaniola. He even left 40 men on Haiti to search for gold and to start the first European colony ever founded in the Americas. It proved to be short-lived, but it preceded the one that Spain founded later at St. Augustine, Florida, by almost 75 years.

Columbus landing at Watling Island. He called the island "San Salvador" and claimed it in the name of the king and queen of Spain.

Columbus returned to Spain in triumph. Taking back with him a few Indians, some parrots, a handful of plants, and some gold ornaments the natives had worn, he was hailed a hero. He convinced Ferdinand and Isabella that he had reached the gates of the Far East, and that gold, spices, and precious jewels lay just beyond, so they financed other voyages on his behalf. Between 1493 and 1504, he made three more trips to the New World. He went on to discover Jamaica and to explore parts of South and Central America. But he never found the gold and other valuables that he had assured the Spanish monarchs he would find.

Columbus died in 1506, a disgraced and broken man. To his dying day, he was convinced he had reached Asia. It never occurred to him that he had discovered a New World. Even after Amerigo Vespucci, an Italian sailing for Portugal, had stated that the land he himself touched in 1497 was indeed an entirely different continent, Columbus held firm to his belief. When new maps were produced in 1507, they showed the New World's name to be America, after Vespucci, without any acknowledgment of Columbus's role.

Name _____ Date _____

Create a Dialogue

When the Arawak Indians of Watling Island first spotted Columbus's ships approaching, they must have excitedly discussed among themselves what was happening and wondered about the strange men who were about to land in their midst.

Do you think the Indians were afraid, or do you think they were more curious than fearful? What do you suppose was racing through their minds at the time? On the lines provided, write a dialogue that might have taken place between several Arawaks as they watched the Spaniards coming ashore.

_____

_____

_____

_____

_____

_____

_____

_____

_____

_____

_____

_____

_____

_____

_____

_____

_____

_____

From Everyday Life: Exploration and Discovery © 2005 Good Year Books.

Name _____ Date _____

Use Context Clues to Complete Sentences

Fill in the blanks in the sentences using the words from the word box.

altered
backing
bound
convoy
emigrate
familiar
fate
fellow
fleet
happenstance
Italian
petitioned
remained
residence
swim

How Christopher Columbus Came to Live in Portugal

Most students are _____ with how Columbus came about discovering the New World. They know he first _____ the king of Portugal and was turned down. They also know that, in the end, he finally received the _____ of the king and queen of Spain.

What most students do not know, however, is how Columbus, an _____, came to live in Portugal. He did not _____ there by chance; his taking up _____ among the Portuguese was a matter of sheer _____. Had not _____ stepped in and _____ the course of history, Christopher Columbus might have _____ in Genoa his entire life.

In brief, here is what happened. In May 1476, Columbus was part of a _____ of Genoese ships _____ for England that was attacked by a combined _____ of French and Portuguese ships. His ship was sunk, but Columbus, although wounded, managed to _____ six miles to the Portuguese shore. Somehow, he made his way to Lisbon and to the welcoming arms of _____ Genoese already living there.

And that is how Christopher Columbus came to live in Portugal.

Name _____ Date _____

Distinguish between Fact and Opinion

In our daily conversations, we often make statements we presume to be factual but which, in reality, are only opinions. In truth, much of what we say while discussing things (e.g., politics) constitutes personal opinions rather than facts.

Can you distinguish between a fact and an opinion? Remember that a fact is something known to be true and that can be proven; an opinion is only a strong belief. With this in mind, indicate on the appropriate line whether each of the statements on this page is a fact or an opinion. Write F for fact and O for opinion.

1. ____ Columbus was more intelligent than most mariners of his day.

2. ____ Columbus believed that Cipango (Japan) was much closer to Europe than it actually is.

3. ____ No one in the early 1400s knew of the existence of North and South America.

4. ____ Columbus was more selfish in his demands for rank and riches than were his fellow explorers.

5. ____ In Columbus's time, sailors were very superstitious concerning the sea.

6. ____ During the long voyage across the Atlantic, Columbus purposely deceived his crews as to the true distance they had covered.

7. ____ Had they mutinied, Columbus's men would have surely killed their leader.

8. ____ The Indians of the New World were better off as a result of their having been "discovered" by Columbus.

9. ____ If Columbus had encountered hostile Indians on Watling Island and he and his men had been killed, America might never have been discovered.

10. ____ The fact that Columbus did not find rich cities and golden palaces proved conclusively that Marco Polo was a liar.

11. ____ Even though Columbus made four voyages to America, he died still believing he had reached Asia.

From Everyday Life: Exploration and Discovery © 2005 Good Year Books.

Name _____ Date _____

Interpret a Bar Graph

Between 1492 and 1502, Columbus made four voyages to the New World. The number of days required to make each crossing depended on such factors as the weather and how long his ships stopped at the Canary Islands before striking out west across the Atlantic Ocean.

The bar graph on this page indicates the number of days each of the four voyages took. Using the information from the graph, answer the questions at the right.

1. Which two voyages more closely approximate each other in length (number of days long)?

   _____

2. What is the mean number of days for the voyages?

   _____

3. What is the range? _____

4. Explain why there is no mode among the numbers.

   _____

   _____

5. Why is there no median? _____

   _____

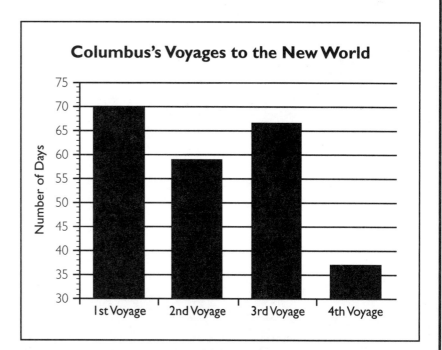

Columbus's Voyages to the New World

From Everyday Life: Exploration and Discovery © 2005 Good Year Books.

CHAPTER 7

The Spanish Conquistadors

"We Spaniards suffer from a disease that only gold can cure." Thus spoke Hernando Cortés, Captain General and conqueror of the Aztec Indians of Mexico. His words might just have easily been uttered by any of the Spanish soldiers of fortune who came to the New World in the 1400s in search of gold, glory, and power. Such soldiers of fortune are referred to in history as *conquistadors*, which in English means "conquerors." Coming from all ranks of Spanish society, they shared one common characteristic: a fanatical desire for gold. How they got it or who got hurt in the process mattered little. Their cruelty toward—and their exploitation of—the natives of Latin America far overshadowed any half-hearted attempts they made at colonization.

Hernando Cortés. Cortés destroyed the civilization of the Aztecs and added Mexico to the Spanish Empire.

The first conquistador of note was Vasco Nuñez de Balboa. In 1513, he crossed the Isthmus of Panama and discovered the Pacific Ocean (well, at least the eastern shore of it), which he named the South Sea. (Magellan would later call it the Pacific Ocean.) Some sources say Balboa shipped 30,000 gold pieces back to the king of Spain, stating that there was more where that came from. News of such wealth created a Spanish "gold rush" that ultimately resulted in Spain gaining control of all of Latin America except Brazil.

Hernando Cortés followed on the heels of Balboa. In April 1519, Cortés and a force of about 700 soldiers landed near Tabasco on the Yucatan Peninsula of Mexico. The Indians who greeted him fought fiercely for awhile to throw the Spaniards back into the sea. Then Cortés ordered the 16 horses he had on board to be brought ashore. This maneuver turned the tide. The Indians had never seen a horse and believed the animal and its rider together constituted one menacing beast. So when they saw rider and horse approaching, they turned and ran into a nearby swamp.

After having been introduced to the horse, the Indians of Tabasco were subdued easily. Cortés made it even easier by telling them—through an interpreter—that he had big guns that were very angry because they (the

From *Everyday Life: Exploration and Discovery* © 2005 Good Year Books.

Indians) had resisted his landing. He further warned them that he had no control over the anger of these weapons and that he never knew when they might speak. To drive home his point, and by prearranged signal, he had the men he left on the ship fire a round of cannon over the heads of the already stunned Indians. Any thought they had of further resistance quickly vanished.

Cortés ordered the Indians of Tabasco to return to their villages, which they did. He also ordered them to destroy their pagan idols and take up the Cross. Before they dispersed, however, they told him of the great Aztec ruler Montezuma (or Moctezuma), who held court at Tenochtitlan, now Mexico City. Montezuma was not only powerful but very rich. His capital, which sat on an island in the middle of the lake, was a city of pyramids, palaces, and, presumably, much gold. It was this prospect of finding gold that turned Cortés's attention in the direction of Tenochtitlan.

Magnificent temples and buildings such as these were characteristic of the Aztec city of Tenochtitlan, present-day Mexico City.

Cortés founded the town of Veracruz and then struck out for the interior of Mexico. Along the way he picked up numerous Indian allies who had been subjected to harsh Aztec rule and who saw the Spaniards as liberators. These Indians also hated and feared the Aztecs because of their religion. The Aztecs worshipped many gods, chief among whom was Huitzilopochtli, the god of war and of the sun. To rise each morning, Huitzilopochtli required the sacrifice of human blood and hearts. Inasmuch as the Indians who allied themselves with Cortés were among those chosen for the sacrificial altar, it is easy to see why they chose to join the Spaniards.

On the march to Tenochtitlan, Cortés defeated large Aztec armies at Tlaxacala and Cholula. The latter was the holy city of the Aztecs, and the Spaniards looted its temples and palaces and killed 3,000 Indian defenders. When the frightened Montezuma heard of the disaster at Cholula, he threw open the gates of his capital and welcomed the invaders.

From Everyday Life: Exploration and Discovery © 2005 Good Year Books.

Cortés had more going for him than just guns, armor, and horses. In the Aztecs' eyes, he represented the fulfillment of a prophecy involving Quetzalcoatl, one of their chief gods. According to legend, after creating life long ago, Quetzalcoatl had disappeared across the vast sea. But the Aztecs believed he would return one day in a large boat. He would be white and he would have a beard. He would then become the supreme leader of the Aztecs. It is easy to see how the Aztecs took Cortés to be Quetzalcoatl.

Francisco Pizarro, the conquistador who defeated the Inca Indians of Peru.

Because Montezuma believed Cortés and his soldiers were gods, he treated them with honor and gave them gifts of gold and jewels. The Aztec emperor then made a grave mistake, he ordered an attack on the Spanish soldiers at Veracruz. In the scuffle, several Spaniards were killed, revealing to the Aztecs that the invaders were not gods but mere mortals like themselves.

When Cortés heard of the attack on Veracruz, he seized Montezuma and made him prisoner. Fierce fighting broke out between the Aztecs and the Spaniards, which, in the end, led to the Spanish conquest of all of Mexico by 1519. During the bloody struggle, Montezuma was killed by his own people, and the once mighty Aztec Empire came to an end.

What Cortés did to the Aztecs of Mexico, a conquistador named Francisco Pizarro did to the Incas of Peru. Pizarro, in fact, was even more cruel and deceitful than his counterpart in Mexico. He thought nothing of seizing and holding the Inca emperor, Atahualpa, for ransom and then murdering him after the ransom was paid.

Francisco Pizarro was born poor. As a youth, he was a swineherd who never learned to read and write. He came to the Americas in 1502 and settled in Hispaniola. In 1513 he accompanied Balboa on his expedition across Panama. Between 1519 and 1523 he was made magistrate of Panama. After Balboa's death, he received a grant of land in Panama and became a farmer.

Pizarro was not satisfied with the life of a farmer. He had heard of the rich empire of the Incas in what is now Peru, and he was consequently struck with "gold fever." In 1528 he went back to Spain and received the backing of King Charles V for an expedition and was appointed governor of Peru. In 1531, he set out from Panama with a force of 180 men and 27 horses.

From *Everyday Life: Exploration and Discovery* © 2005 Good Year Books.

From Everyday Life: Exploration and Discovery © 2005 GoodYear Books.

Pizarro found the Incan Empire in a state of civil war and confusion. Atahualpa had recently rebelled against his brother, Huascar, and had seized the throne. Aware of the Incas' weakness, Pizarro took Atahualpa prisoner and demanded a huge ransom for his release. He told the Incas that he would free their emperor only after they filled a certain room to the top with gold. Obediently, Incas loyal to the emperor began bringing gold to Pizarro. They brought golden statues, trays, jewelry, and other items. But when the room was filled, Pizarro tried Atahualpa on some trumped-up charge and had him strangled. The conquest of the Incan Empire followed quickly thereafter.

Many other conquistadors followed Cortés and Pizarro. One was Francisco Vasquez de Coronado, who searched unsuccessfully for the mythical Seven Cities of Cibola. In 1540, he marched thousands of miles from Mexico into what later became the southwestern United States. His mission was to find seven Indian cities reputed to contain houses and buildings filled with gold. After two and a half months, however, all Coronado found were Zuni Indian pueblos (houses) that, when viewed from afar with the sun beating down on them, shown like gold. In the process of looking for the cities, Coronado discovered the Grand Canyon and explored much of the American Southwest.

Another Spanish explorer was Hernando de Soto. In 1541 he marched westward from Florida (discovered in 1513 by Juan Ponce de Leon) in search of gold. He found none, but he did become the first white man to discover the Mississippi River. De Soto died one year later. In order to conceal the fact that he was not a god, as the Indians of the region believed, de Soto's men weighted his body with stones and buried him in the mighty river he had discovered.

Last, but not least, was Ferdinand Magellan. He set sail from Spain in 1519 with a fleet of five ships and 240 men. His goal was to find the elusive western route to the Indies. In the course of his voyage, he sailed around the tip of South America and on to the Philippine Islands. Although he himself was killed in the Philippines in a battle with natives, one of his ships managed to return to Spain in September 1522. Magellan's expedition proved conclusively that the world was round and that it was much larger than Columbus and others had thought it to be.

Spain's explorations and conquests stagger the imagination. Her empire included Mexico, Central America, California, Florida, the Philippines, the southwestern United States, and all of South America except Brazil, which the Portuguese controlled. From her possessions in Latin America, gold and silver poured into Spain's coffers, making her the richest and most powerful nation in Europe for many years thereafter.

Name _____ Date _____

Solve Some Exploration Word Problems

Solve the four word problems on the page. Write the correct answers on the blank lines. Space is provided for you to work each problem.

1. In the first quarter of the 1500s, Spain imported about 25,000 pounds of gold from the New World. Between 1541 and 1560, the amount of gold imports increased to 150,000 pounds. What percent increase does the latter amount represent?

   _____ %

2. Between the years 1601 and 1620, Spanish gold imports had dwindled to about 40,000 pounds. Therefore, between 1560 and 1620, imports had decreased _____ times.

3. Ferdinand Magellan was killed in the Philippines on April 27, 1521. One of his ships, however, managed to complete the voyage around the world, arriving in Spain on September 6, 1522. How many weeks elapsed between Magellan's death and the completion of the expedition? (Round your answer.)

   _____ weeks

4. Ferdinand Magellan left Spain on September 20, 1519, with five ships and 240 men. Juan Sebastian del Cano, who commanded the *Victoria,* the only ship to complete the journey, arrived back in Spain with a total of 18 men. What percent of Magellan's original crew returned?

   _____ %

From *Everyday Life: Exploration and Discovery* © 2005 GoodYear Books.

Name _____ Date _____

Write a Letter to the Editor

Suppose that newspapers were commonplace during the Age of Exploration and Discovery and that you are a Spanish citizen deeply troubled by your country's treatment of the Indians of Mexico, Central America, and South America.

Write a letter to the editor of your local newspaper criticizing such treatment. You can learn more about the subject by consulting an encyclopedia or any book dealing with exploration and conquest.

October 25, 1530

Dear Editor,

_____

_____

_____

_____

_____

_____

_____

_____

_____

_____

_____

_____

_____

_____

_____

_____

_____

_____

_____

Sincerely,

_____

(Your Name)

Name _____ Date _____

Solve a Conquistador Puzzle

Fill in the sentences for clues to complete the puzzle about the Spanish conquistadors.

```
          C _ _ _ _ _
      _ _ _ _ O _
        _ _ N _ _ _ _ _ _
      _ _ _ Q _ _ _
    _ _ _ _ _ U _ _
        _ I _ _ _ _
      _ _ _ _ S _
        _ _ T _ _ _
        _ A _ _ _ _ _ _
    _ _ _ _ _ D _
      _ _ _ _ O _ _
        _ _ R _ _ _ _ _ _
          S _ _ _ _
```

1. Mexico was conquered by Hernando _____.

2. _____ discovered the Pacific Ocean.

3. _____ was the emperor of the Aztecs.

4. The word *conquistador* means _____.

5. _____ was the ruler of the Incas at the time of the Spanish conquest.

6. Some conquistadors hoped to find the Seven Cities of _____.

7. The _____ were the Peruvian Indians conquered by the Spaniards.

8. Hernando Cortés defeated the _____ of Mexico.

9. _____ led the first expedition to sail around the world.

10. Juan Ponce de Leon is given credit for discovering _____.

11. The Mississippi River was discovered by Hernando _____.

12. _____ explored the American southwest and discovered the Grand Canyon.

13. The conquistadors claimed much of the New World for _____.

From Everyday Life: Exploration and Discovery © 2005 Good Year Books.

Name _____ Date _____

Whip Up Some Tortillas

Today we enjoy many foods that are usually associated with Mexico. Four of these are tamales, enchiladas, tacos, and tortillas. But did you know that some of these foods were being prepared by the Aztecs long before the arrival of the Spaniards?

One early food prepared by Aztec wives were tortillas. As you probably know, tortillas are flat, round cakes usually made of cornmeal. They can, however, be just as easily fashioned from either ground hominy meal or regular, all-purpose flour. Aztec women made their meal for tortillas by grinding maize, or corn.

Below is a recipe for simple tortillas that probably differs little from the way the Aztecs made them long ago. Ask your parent(s) or guardian(s) to help you "whip up a batch."

Here is all you need:

1 cup corn meal

1-1/2 cups boiling water

1/4 tsp salt

1 can of Mexican-style beans

1 small can of tomato sauce

Cooked sausage or ground meat (if desired)

Here is what you do:

1. Add boiling water to a cup of cornmeal.

2. Combine to make a paste.

3. Knead paste into small balls and roll as thin as possible with a rolling pin.

4. Fry on a dry griddle or skillet. Cook about 1 minute. Turn over and continue cooking for another minute. Brown speckles will appear.

5. Top with Mexican-style beans, tomato sauce, and sausage or ground meat, if you like.

CHAPTER 8

The French in the New World

In the 1500s no European nation seriously challenged Spain's claim to a vast portion of the Americas. Portugal, of course, had taken control of Brazil, but beyond that, Spain was generally free to act as she chose. Mexico, Central America, and most of South America and the West Indies were under the Spanish flag. So were Florida and much of what would later become the southwestern United States.

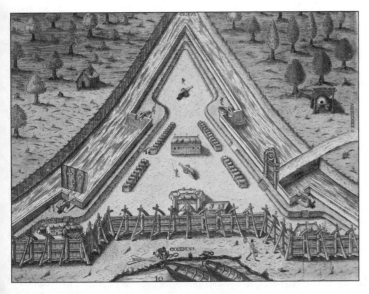

Fort Caroline, built by the French near present-day Jacksonville, Florida, in 1564.

Spanish control over so much of the New World was contested only in Florida. Although Juan Ponce de Leon had claimed "La Florida" for Spain in 1513, this did not prevent the French from making a colonization effort there themselves. Their confidence was boosted by the success of French pirate ships in outgunning slow-moving Spanish galleons laden with gold and silver from Mexico and Peru. The French reasoned they would have little difficulty wresting control of Florida from their Spanish neighbor. They had even begun to brazenly call La Florida "Newe France."

At first, things looked promising. Jean Ribault left France in 1562 with three ships and 150 men. Crossing the Atlantic in two and a half months, he landed at the mouth of the St. Johns River near where Jacksonville stands today. He erected a stone column as proof that he had claimed the land for France, whereupon he sailed northward to present-day South Carolina. There he established Charlesfort, which he named in honor of King Charles IX of France. Charlesfort was soon abandoned, but Rene de Laudonniere, who had sailed with Ribault, later founded Fort Caroline on the St. Johns River in 1564.

The French presence at Fort Caroline disturbed the Spanish for two reasons. First, it posed a threat to Spain, which had already laid claim to Florida. Second, the French who had come to colonize Florida were Huguenots, or French Protestants. The Spanish were devout Roman Catholics who resented the presence of Protestants on their land. The task of throwing out the French was assigned to Pedro Menendez de Aviles, newly appointed

From *Everyday Life: Exploration and Discovery* © 2005 Good Year Books.

governor of La Florida and captain-general of the Spanish Fleet. In addition to driving out the French, Menendez planned to establish a permanent colony in Florida. With that in mind, he founded St. Augustine on September 8, 1565.

A short time later, Menendez marched on Fort Caroline from St. Augustine at the height of a hurricane. His men could not believe what their commander had ordered them to do. But their attack during the middle of what the Indians called *Huracan,* or "Great Evil Wind Spirit," caught the sleepy French by surprise. Menendez killed more than 200 Huguenots in the early morning assault. He spared a few women and children, and Laudonniere, who commanded the fort, managed to swim with others to the safety of a French ship anchored nearby.

In the meantime, Jean Ribault was on his way to St. Augustine to attack the Spanish post there. However, unacquainted with the ways of hurricanes, he managed to either lose or wreck all his ships in the waters just south of the new Spanish settlement. In the weeks that followed, he and some 350 of his men were slaughtered at an inlet that came to be called *Matanzas,* the Spanish word for "slaughtering place." The capture of Fort Caroline and the killing of Ribault's men at Matanzas ended all French hopes of colonizing Florida.

The French fared better farther north. There, their claims to territory in North America were based on the voyage of an Italian navigator named Giovanni da Verranzano. In 1524, Verranzano, sailing in the service of France, explored the Atlantic coast and discovered both New York and Narragansett bays. He is believed to have sailed as far north as Newfoundland.

Verranzano was looking for the Northwest Passage. The Northwest Passage was a supposed sea route from the Atlantic to the Pacific Ocean. Such a waterway does exist, but it is too winding and too choked with ice to make it practical for all except icebreaking ships. Still, European countries during the Age of Exploration and Discovery spent considerable time and effort trying to find the passage. For his part, Verranzano thought he had found the passage when he came upon Pamlico Sound at Cape Hatteras, North Carolina. The waters he saw were for many years later referred to on maps as "Verranzano's Sea."

Ten years later, another Frenchman sailed to North America in search of gold and precious metals and to find the Northwest Passage. His name was Jacques Cartier. In 1534, he landed at Newfoundland and claimed all of Canada for France. Cartier did not accept "Verranzano's Sea" as the way to Asia. Instead, he thought a strait directly through the continent lay somewhere between Cape Breton and Newfoundland.

One year later, Cartier made a second trip to North America. This time he discovered the St. Lawrence River. Mistakenly thinking that Indian villages as rich as those found by the Spanish in Mexico and Peru lay inland, Cartier sailed 125 miles up the river to the Indian village of Hochelaga (later Montreal). There he and his men were welcomed by the Iroquois, who proved to be courteous and friendly. The Iroquois introduced their guests to a food they had never seen or tasted before: corn. The French in turn introduced the Iroquois to hardtack (a very hard biscuit) and red wine. The Indians, however, would partake of neither. In their opinion, the French were eating wood and drinking blood!

The French explorer Jacques Cartier. Cartier discovered the St. Lawrence River in 1535.

Cartier made a final visit to the New World in 1541. This time he established a settlement, but it lasted only a year. In three trips, the disappointed explorer had found neither gold nor the Northwest Passage. Even his colony had failed. Were his explorations in vain? Not at all; by discovering the St. Lawrence River, he had found the gateway to the interior of the continent—a gateway that led to the Great Lakes and the establishment of a lucrative fur trade.

After Cartier's expeditions, French interest in North America dwindled for more than half a century. Internal affairs and European politics demanded the time and attention of the French monarchy. Not until 1608 did France once again turn serious attention to the New World. In that year, Samuel de Champlain, who had made an earlier trip to Canada in 1603, founded Quebec. Champlain was more interested in establishing a permanent colony than in finding gold, and for this reason he is often called the "Father of New France."

Champlain was a good leader, but he made a terrible mistake when he sided with the Algonquin and Huron Indians in a war against the Iroquois. Thereafter, the Iroquois were a bitter enemy, later joining the English and Dutch in their efforts to drive French settlers out of North America. Champlain also did nothing to aid his cause when he personally killed two Iroquois chiefs with his own musket.

From *Everyday Life: Exploration and Discovery* © 2005 Good Year Books.

On one raid against the Iroquois, Champlain discovered the large lake situated between New York and Vermont that today bears his name. Still, his getting involved in a tribal war, coupled with an influx of French settlers, caused friction between his people and the Indians of New France. Even the Hurons, on whose side Champlain had fought, turned bitter against the French. This is best seen in the story of Etienne Brule.

Etienne Brule was a young Frenchman who accompanied Champlain on a number of expeditions. Because he had lived among the Hurons and knew their ways and language, Brule was invaluable as a guide. He did not realize, however, that the Hurons' attitude toward the French had slowly changed. He assumed that if he ventured into their territory he would be welcomed as usual. He was wrong. When he stopped to visit his former friends while on his way back from an exploration, he was seized and killed.

Compared to the English, few French settlers actually came to New France. Farming never took hold, and most efforts were concentrated on the fur and fishing trades. In spite of their numbers remaining relatively small, the French explored and claimed a large part of North America. In 1682, Robert de La Salle canoed down the Mississippi River to the Gulf of Mexico. As a result, he claimed all the inland area of North America for France. He named the region Louisiana in honor of his king. Many years later, the United States would purchase this huge chunk of territory from France.

A fort built by Samuel de Champlain near the St. Lawrence River in Canada. Champlain founded the city of Quebec in 1608.

Name _____ Date _____

Recall Information You Have Read

Without looking back over the chapter, see how well you can explain the role played in North America by each of the explorers listed.

1. Jean Ribault

_____

_____

2. Giovanni da Verranzano

_____

_____

3. Jacques Cartier

_____

_____

4. Samuel de Champlain

_____

_____

5. Robert de La Salle

_____

_____

6. Rene de Laudonniere

_____

_____

7. Pedro Menendez de Aviles

_____

_____

From Everyday Life: Exploration and Discovery © 2005 Good Year Books.

Name _____   Date _____

Research the Great Lakes

How familiar are you with the Great Lakes region, which, as you learned in chapter 8, was discovered and settled by the French during the Age of Exploration and Discovery? Consult an encyclopedia, almanac, or other source to answer questions about these five important waterways.

1. The five Great Lakes are _____, _____, _____, _____, and _____.

2. Lake _____ is the only Great Lake that lies wholly in the United States.

3. The largest of the lakes is Lake _____.

4. Lake _____ is the smallest of the Great Lakes.

5. What is the total area of Lake Michigan in square miles? _____. How deep is it at its greatest depth? _____

6. Lake Superior has a total area of _____ square miles. At its greatest depth, it is _____ feet deep.

7. Lake Michigan borders four states. They are _____, _____, _____, and _____.

8. There are six large port cities on Lake Michigan. Three of these are _____, _____, and _____.

9. What is the total area of the five lakes combined? _____.

10. Why were the Great Lakes so important to the growth and development of early America?

_____

_____

_____

Name _____ Date _____

Create a Dialogue

To the Indians of the Americas, European explorers and settlers had strange ways. They talked "funny," wore too many clothes, and ate and drank the most unusual things. With the latter in mind, create a conversation that might have taken place between several Iroquois children upon observing the French eating hardtack and drinking red wine, which, as has already been mentioned, they took to be wood and blood.

Be creative in developing your dialogue. Put yourself in the shoes of the Iroquois children and imagine what they would say among themselves as they giggled and looked on.

_____
_____
_____
_____
_____
_____
_____
_____
_____
_____
_____
_____
_____
_____
_____
_____
_____
_____
_____
_____
_____
_____
_____
_____

From Everyday Life: Exploration and Discovery © 2005 Good Year Books.

Name _____ Date _____

Arrange Events in Chronological Order

Using the numbers 1 through 13, place the events listed in the order in which they occurred. Refer to chapters 5 through 8 for appropriate dates.

_____ De Soto discovers the Mississippi River.

_____ Magellan leads the first expedition to sail around the world.

_____ La Salle sails down the Mississippi River to the Gulf of Mexico.

_____ Diaz sails around the Cape of Good Hope.

_____ Menendez founds St. Augustine.

_____ Balboa discovers the Pacific Ocean.

_____ Champlain founds Quebec.

_____ Da Gama sails around Africa to India.

_____ Columbus discovers America.

_____ Verranzano searches for the Northwest Passage.

_____ Pizarro conquers the Incan Empire.

_____ Cartier discovers the St. Lawrence River.

_____ Coronado searches for the Seven Cities of Cibola.

Extension: In your opinion, which two of the above events had the greatest impact on the course of history? Explain your answer.

_____

_____

_____

_____

_____

_____

_____

From Everyday Life: Exploration and Discovery © 2005 Good Year Books.

CHAPTER 9

The English in America

The only clues were a few abandoned chests and the word *Croatoan* carved on a tree. No fort. No crude shelters. No crops. Nothing. Some 150 settlers had simply disappeared.

What had happened to the "Lost Colony" on Roanoke Island? No one knows for sure. The leader of the group, John White, had returned to England for badly needed supplies soon after the colony was established in 1587. Unable to come back until 1590, he was shocked to find no trace of the colonists. Included among the missing was John White's granddaughter, Virginia Dare, the first English child born in North America.

Drawing of Croatoan Indians of Roanoke Island off North Carolina. Many historians believe the Croatoans were somehow tied to the disappearance of the Lost Colony.

White's attempt at founding a permanent English settlement at Roanoke Island followed two unsuccessful efforts by Sir Walter Raleigh. Raleigh's first group almost starved before being picked up and taken back to England. Of the second group, none remained alive when White's band landed there on July 22, 1587.

Historians differ as to what fate befell the so-called Lost Colony. Some believe that Croatoan was a nearby island to which the settlers moved and on which they later died. Others hold that Croatoan was the name of an Indian tribe whose members either killed White's group or who intermarried with the English, erasing the settlers' identity.

The attempt to establish a colony on Roanoke Island came almost 100 years after the English first laid claim to land in the New World. In 1497, an Italian navigator name Giovanni Caboto (in English, John Cabot), sailing in the service of England, explored present-day New England and parts of the Canadian coast. He found no gold, silver, jewels, or spices, but, like Columbus five years earlier, he was convinced he had reached the fringes of Cathay (China). He was wrong, of course, but his expedition at least gave England a basis for challenging other European powers for control of North America.

From *Everyday Life: Exploration and Discovery* © 2005 Good Year Books.

After the failure of the Roanoke Colony, 20 years passed before the English made another attempt to found a permanent settlement in North America. In 1607 they succeeded at Jamestown, Virginia, but only because of the strong leadership of a soldier and adventurer named John Smith. Had Smith not emerged and taken control of the colony in 1608, Jamestown might have become another Roanoke.

Never was a group of settlers more unsuited to the task of founding a colony than those who landed at Jamestown on May 14, 1607. Of 100 men and 4 boys, roughly half were gentlemen, or landed gentry, unaccustomed to work and spoiled from a life of ease. Most came with only the clothes on their backs, their sole mission being to search for gold. And search for gold they did, at the exclusion of trying to figure out how they would survive in a harsh and unfriendly environment. Left to their own devices, they would have all perished had not John Smith appeared.

As it was, many of the first Jamestown settlers did die. The site they chose for a settlement was on swampy ground and rife with mosquitoes, and the drinking water was unfit to consume. Malaria, dysentery, and pneumonia quickly took their toll. By the end of the first winter, only 38 of the original 104 settlers were alive.

Pocahontas saving John Smith's life. Some historians doubt if the incident really happened.

John Smith became the leader of the colony and immediately established a set of rules. He told the "gentlemen" who survived that terrible first year that if they wanted to eat, they had to work. Although "work" was no doubt an alien concept to them, the men set to work building houses and a fort. They also dug wells and planted corn, which friendly Indians had shown them how to grow. Until the corn ripened, Smith kept the group alive by hunting for meat and trading with the Indians for food.

It was on one of Smith's hunting trips that he was captured by hostile Indians and threatened with death. By Smith's own account, his head was at

From Everyday Life: Exploration and Discovery © 2005 Good Year Books.

the point of being bashed in by several surly Indians when Pocahontas, the daughter of Chief Powhatan, stepped in and saved his life. Whether this story is true is open to conjecture. Smith later related a similar tale of being saved by an Indian girl in what is now New Hampshire. How many times could one man be saved in the same manner and under similar circumstances?

John Smith might have possibly stretched the truth a bit, but it is a fact that his leadership and determination saved the fledgling colony at Jamestown. He himself returned to England in 1609 after being wounded in a gunpowder explosion, but the colony, in spite of disease and Indian attacks, not only survived but prospered. Newly arrived settlers eventually turned the entire Virginia region into a thriving colony based on the growing of tobacco.

Thirteen years after the founding of Jamestown, another group of English settlers arrived in America. These were the Pilgrims. In England, they were known as "Separatists" because of their desire to completely separate themselves from the Church of England, which they viewed as being too much like the Roman Catholic Church in beliefs and ceremony.

Because they were persecuted for their beliefs, some Separatists fled to Holland. There they lived in peace, but many among them were not altogether happy. They watched helplessly as their children began to grow up more Dutch than English. The fear that their children would forsake their English ways convinced a small number of Separatists to sail for America in 1620. Because the voyage across the Atlantic was a kind of pilgrimage, the Separatists thereafter were called Pilgrims.

The Pilgrims arrived at Plymouth, Massachusetts, on December 11, 1620. Although they quickly built a Common House and a number of huts for shelter, their first winter in America was difficult. More than half of the 103 that had sailed over in the *Mayflower* died of sickness and lack of food within a few months. A miracle was needed to save the remainder from the same fate.

Enter Squanto and other friendly Indians of the Wampanoag tribe. Squanto had been to England (possibly taken there by earlier traders), and he

Squanto of the Wampanoag tribe. With his tribe's help, the Pilgrims were able to survive their first harsh winter in Plymouth.

From *Everyday Life: Exploration and Discovery* © 2005 GoodYear Books.

spoke English quite well. He served as interpreter for the Pilgrims, and, with the help of other members of his tribe, taught the newcomers how to grow corn, beans, and pumpkins. He also taught them how to hunt for game and to catch herring for fertilizer. Thanks to his help, Plymouth Colony got off to a sound footing.

Meanwhile, back in England, a much larger group seeking religious freedom was soon to embark for America. They were the Puritans, so-called because they wanted to "purify" or rid the Church of England of such things as altars, statues, and even candles. (The Pilgrims were originally part of the Puritan group, but they chose to separate themselves entirely from the English church.) Faced with persecution at the hands of the king, many of the Puritans fled to New England in 1630.

The towns and settlements founded by the Puritans came to be called the Massachusetts Bay Colony. The Puritans were like the Pilgrims in that they came to America for religious freedom. But most resemblance ended there. Whereas the Pilgrims were more accepting of others, the Puritans were strict and intolerant. Anyone who disagreed with Puritan authorities ran the risk of being driven out or even put to death. It is ironic that the Puritans, who came to America for religious freedom, were never willing to grant this freedom to others.

More English settlers came to America in the years following the Puritans' arrival. By 1732, settlements dotted the Atlantic Seaboard from New England to Georgia. In time, these settlements grew to become the original 13 colonies. They were inhabited by hardy immigrants who braved a dangerous ocean voyage in search of a better life. Most came, of course, for religious freedom. But others came for land or simply for adventure. Still others came to escape political persecution in Europe. Whatever their reasons for coming, these original English settlers laid the foundation for what later became the United States.

If there was one thing that distinguished English settlers from their Spanish and French counterparts, it was that they came in greater numbers and they came to stay. The Spanish, as you have seen, were mainly interested in gold and silver. Although a handful of French were determined to make it as farmers, they primarily focused their attention on the fur trade. But the English seemed determined to become permanent residents from the start. This was one of the reasons why they, instead of their rivals, ended up with control of the continent.

From Everyday Life: Exploration and Discovery © 2005 Good Year Books.

Name _____ Date _____

Write a Lead Paragraph for the *London Digest*

Suppose daily newspapers existed in the 1500s and that you are a roving reporter for the *London Digest*. Also imagine that you are with John White in 1590 when he discovered that the Roanoke Colony had vanished. Your assignment as reporter is to write a story on the disappearance of the colony.

On the lines provided, write the lead paragraph to your story. Be sure to include answers to the five "W" questions (Who? What? When? Where? and Why?) that are characteristic of a good lead paragraph. The headlines have been written for you.

The London Digest

★ ★ ★ ★ ★ **August 18, 1580** ★ ★ ★ ★ ★

No Trace Found of Roanoke Colony
Word on Tree Holds Only Clue

_____

_____

_____

_____

_____

_____

_____

_____

_____

_____

_____

_____

_____

_____

_____

_____

From *Everyday Life: Exploration and Discovery* © 2005 Good Year Books.

Name _____ Date _____

Draw Conclusions about the Lost Colony

In the previous activity, you were asked to write the lead paragraph of an article about the Lost Colony of Roanoke that might have appeared in a London newspaper of the 1500s. Now, after thinking about the strange circumstances surrounding the case, write what you think happened to the colony and its inhabitants. Support your theory with what you consider logical conclusions.

To make the fate of the Lost Colony even more puzzling, there is said to be a group of Native Americans in the region today who go by the tribal name *Croatoan*. Even more interesting is that most of them have English last names. Can you explain how this might have come about?

_____

_____

_____

_____

_____

_____

_____

_____

_____

_____

_____

_____

_____

_____

_____

_____

_____

_____

_____

Name _____ Date _____

Answer Questions about the *Mayflower Compact*

Before the Pilgrims even left ship to establish their settlement at Plymouth, they drew up the first written plan for self-government in America. This plan was called the *Mayflower Compact.*

Look up the *Mayflower Compact* in a textbook, an encyclopedia, or a book dealing with the period. Then answer the questions on this page.

1. On what date was the agreement signed? _____

2. Where was the *Mayflower* anchored at the time?
_____

3. Who was the king of England when the *Mayflower* sailed for America? _____

4. What circumstances led to the framing (drawing up) of the compact?
_____
_____
_____

5. How many men signed the agreement? _____

6. Why do you think women aboard the *Mayflower* were not allowed to participate in drawing up the plan of government? Do you think they were upset by their exclusion? Why or why not?
_____
_____
_____

7. What American tradition was established by the *Mayflower Compact?*
_____

8. After drawing up and signing the *Mayflower Compact,* who did the Pilgrims elect as their first governor?
_____

From Everyday Life: Exploration and Discovery © 2005 Good Year Books.

Name _____   Date _____

Fill in a Map of the 13 Colonies

I n a text or an encyclopedia, find a map showing the original English colonies in America. Then fill in the map below with the name of each. Also include within each boundary the date when the colony was established, along with the name of the person or group responsible for its founding. Fill in each colony with a different color.

CHAPTER 10

The Dutch and Others Join the Race

Ｎew York City is a huge place. Today there are more than 7,000,000 people who call it home. It is by far the largest city in the United States.

The Dutch bought what became New York City from the Manhattan Indians for the astronomical sum of $24—well, $24 in guilders, the Dutch currency, which equaled 1½ pounds of silver. And they did not even have to pay in hard cash! Instead, the Manhattans were delighted to accept payment in the form of hatchets, mirrors, beads, and other trinkets, as well as in a variety of brightly colored cloths.

Were the Manhattans gullible to sell an entire island for a handful of trinkets? Not at all. They sold their land, of which they had plenty, for objects they valued. They had accepted such objects in exchange for furs since 1609, the year the Dutch arrived in America. The Dutch valued the furs, the Indians valued the hatchets and trinkets, and both were happy with the arrangement.

As was true of the English and the French, Dutch interest in North America stemmed from a desire to find the Northwest Passage. In 1609, they hired Henry Hudson, an English sea captain, to find the much-desired waterway. Hudson, of course, did not find what he was looking for, but he did discover and sail up the river that today bears his name. His expedition gave Holland claim to land in the New World. Hudson reported back to his superiors in Holland that the land he explored was good and that the woods teemed with fur-bearing animals. He also learned that the Native Americans who lived there were willing to trap and sell these animals at a cheap price. His report moved Dutch merchants to form a trading company called the Dutch West India Company. Its purpose was to settle the land and establish a thriving fur trade with the Indians who resided there.

Henry Hudson, whose expedition in 1609 gave Holland claim to land in the New World.

From *Everyday Life: Exploration and Discovery* © 2005 GoodYear Books.

One year after his expedition for the Dutch, Hudson sailed back to America, this time in the service of his native England. Once again he was searching for the Northwest Passage. This time he thought he had found it when he sailed into a very large bay in what is now Canada. This bay later came to be called Hudson Bay after its discoverer.

It is now that the story of Henry Hudson turns tragic. Trapped in ice on the bay and forced to spend the winter locked in, he and his crew almost starved. When spring came in 1611, however, Hudson's spirits revived, and he wanted to continue his exploration farther west. His crew refused, and they mutinied and took control of the ship. What the mutineers did afterward is a black mark in English history. Giving them no food and water, the rebels forced Hudson, his son John, and seven loyal seamen into a small boat and set it adrift in the large bay. They were never heard from again.

Meanwhile, back on Manhattan Island and its surrounding areas, Dutch traders who had been there since 1609 were soon to be joined by Dutch settlers. In 1623, the settlement of New Amsterdam was founded on the lower half of the island by 31 families from Leyden, Holland. These families had no interest in the fur trade or in searching for gold. They also gave no thought to finding a passage to Asia. They came to America to build homes and to make a permanent life for themselves.

New Amsterdam and other Dutch settlements in the New York area came to be called New Netherland. By way of explanation, the proper name for the home of the Dutch people is the *Netherlands,* a word meaning "Low Countries." *Holland,* the name formerly used, really applies only to the country's two main western provinces. The word *Dutch* comes from the German "dutsch" and refers to the main language of the country. (You are probably familiar with the Pennsylvania Dutch. They are not Dutch descendants at all, coming instead from southwestern Germany.) Most Dutch prefer to call themselves either Netherlanders or Hollanders.

The first governor of New Netherland arrived in 1626. He was Peter Minuet, a German who had moved to the Netherlands as a young man. It was Minuet who negotiated the official purchase of Manhattan Island from the Indians shortly after assuming his post. It was also Minuet who ordered Fort Amsterdam built to protect the colony on the one side not bordered by water. Fort Amsterdam flourished and in time became the city of New York.

After five years, Peter Minuet fell out of favor with the Dutch West India Company and was recalled to the Netherlands. He was back in America, however,

in 1638. This time he led a Swedish expedition that founded a colony near where Wilmington, Delaware, stands today. He called the settlement Fort Christiana, after the Swedish queen who had enlisted his services. Shortly after helping the Swedes start their settlement, Peter Minuet drowned at sea during a hurricane.

Peter Stuyvesant, the governor of New Netherland, who was resented by the Dutch inhabitants of the colony.

Fort Christiana was short-lived. In 1655, it was taken over by the Dutch and made a part of New Netherland. Then, 10 years later, New Netherland itself was taken over by the English. The story of how that came about is worthy of note.

After Peter Minuet was called home to Holland, New Netherland had several governors, the last of whom was Peter Stuyvesant. Stuyvesant was an old soldier who had lost a leg in battle. His enemies, of whom he had quite a few, called him "Peg-Leg." Some even referred to him as "Old Silver Nails" because he had driven silver nails at various places into his wooden leg.

The people of New Amsterdam and its surrounding areas resented Peter Stuyvesant for his high-handed ways. He treated them like soldiers and he levied new taxes to increase the size of the fort at New Amsterdam. It is not surprising, therefore, that when four English warships appeared in the harbor of New Amsterdam one day in 1664 and their commander announced his intention of seizing control of the colony, not many Dutch settlers heeded Stuyvesant's call to assemble and defend the fort. Why should they come to the aid of a governor they loathed, they reasoned? Why should they fight the British, who promised them self-government and the right to continue to worship as they pleased? They were more than willing to submit to English rule.

Faced with the facts, Peter Stuyvesant could do nothing but give in. The English took control of New Netherland without ceremony, and life went on much as it had before. The only change that took place was in the name of the colony and the city where the fort stood. New Netherland became New York and New Amsterdam became New York City. Both were named for the Duke of York, the brother of the English king, Charles II.

From *Everyday Life: Exploration and Discovery* © 2005 Good Year Books.

The Dutch who lived in the New York area were a liberal people. They welcomed all nationalities and religious faiths. While governor, Peter Stuyvesant had tried to persecute Quakers and Jews, but the residents of what was then New Amsterdam pressured him into letting them remain and worship freely. In addition to Quakers and Jews, a large number of Huguenots, Lutherans, and Catholics lived and prospered in the little town.

The Dutch created a lifestyle unique among early American settlers. They were a sociable people whose houses had small porches with benches that welcomed all passersby who desired to stop and chat. To further encourage conversation, the front doors of Dutch houses were divided into halves that opened separately. A member of the household could stand at the open part and chat for hours, leaving the bottom part closed to prevent stray animals from wandering inside.

Skittles, or ninepins, a game brought to the New World by the Dutch. Skittles was an early form of bowling.

The Dutch were also a happy people. They cherished good food and a good time. They were especially fond of outdoor activities. Skating, coasting, and sailing were favorite amusements. Another was a form of bowling called skittles, or ninepins. Ninepins was played outdoors on lawns. In time it evolved into our modern game of bowling.

Although the Dutch lost out to the English in North America, they made their presence felt elsewhere during the Age of Exploration and Discovery. They took the Spice Islands, Ceylon (Sri Lanka), and Malacca (now part of Malaysia) from Portugal, and they wrested control of Sumatra from England. They also established a colony at the southern tip of Africa in 1652.

The Age of Exploration and Discovery that began in the 1600s had a profound effect on Europe and the rest of the world. In chapter 11, you will learn of the many changes that came about as a result of this important period.

From Everyday Life: Exploration and Discovery © 2005 Good Year Books.

Name _____ Date _____

Write an Eyewitness Account

Imagine yourself a Dutch settler looking on as Peter Minuet negotiated the purchase of Manhattan from the Indians who owned the island. Write an eyewitness account of the dialogue that might have taken place between the governor and the various chiefs in attendance.

From Everyday Life: Exploration and Discovery © 2005 Good Year Books.

Name _____ Date _____

Solve Another Exploration Puzzle

ACROSS

4 First governor of New Netherland

5 _____ Stuyvesant

7 Former name for the Netherlands

9 The Netherlands, the Low _____

13 King Charles's brother, the _____ of York

14 Peter Minuet's nationality

15 Twenty-four _____, the price paid for Manhattan

DOWN

1 Henry _____ who sailed for both the Netherlands and England

2 Where Fort Christiana was located

3 What Sri Lanka was once called

6 _____ Island, where New Amsterdam sprang up

8 Dutch monetary unit

10 The Dutch West _____ Company

11 Where the settlers of Fort Christiana were from

12 Early form of Dutch bowling

From Everyday Life: Exploration and Discovery © 2005 Good Year Books.

Name _____   Date _____

Solve Some Population Math

Although Spain claimed Florida in 1519, the remainder of North America was colonized by four European countries: England, France, Holland, and Sweden. The chart opposite breaks down the estimated population of each country's colonies in 1650. Use the data from the chart to answer these questions, and write the correct answers on the appropriate lines. Space is provided for you to work each problem.

Colonial Settlements	Population
English colonies	50,000
New France (Canada)	10,000
New Netherland	9,000
New Sweden	1,000

1. What was the combined population of the European colonies?

   _____

2. What percent of the total number of settlers in North America did each of the colonies represent? (Round your answers.)

   English colonies _____ %

   New France _____ %

   New Netherland _____ %

   New Sweden _____ %

From Everyday Life: Exploration and Discovery © 2005 Good Year Books.

Name _____ Date _____

Make a Shoe-Box Diorama

The Swedes, who established a short-lived colony at Fort Christiana in present-day Delaware, are usually credited with introducing the log cabin to America. With this in mind, make a shoe-box diorama depicting a scene normally associated with life in and around a log cabin.

Materials That Will Be Helpful Include:

1. A large shoe box

2. Modeling clay or small figurines of people and animals

3. Construction paper

4. Cardboard

5. Watercolors, crayons, or markers

6. Scissors

7. Glue or paste

On the lines below, write a paragraph describing the scene depicted in your diorama.

_____

_____

_____

_____

_____

_____

_____

_____

_____

_____

_____

_____

_____

CHAPTER II

Exploration and Discovery Bring Change

One hot day in the summer of 1619, a lone Dutch ship stopped at Jamestown, Virginia. It would have attracted little attention had it not been for its unusual cargo. Aboard the vessel were 20 Africans that the captain of the ship, a mysterious man named Jope, hoped to trade for food.

How this Captain Jope had come in possession of the Africans is not clear. Rumors persisted that he had attacked a Spanish slave ship somewhere on the high seas and confiscated its human cargo. Whatever the source, this small group of Africans represented the first blacks to be brought to North America. By the time of the U.S. Civil War in 1861, their numbers would grow from 20 to more than 20 million.

Captain Jope's 20 Africans were not sold as slaves but as indentured servants. (Indentured servants were persons who gained their freedom after working without pay for a prescribed number of years.) But the die was cast. After 1619, shipload after shipload of blacks were captured along the African west coast and kept in "forts" until they could be transported to America. No thought was given to selling them as indentured servants. On the contrary, they were all to be sold as slaves to the highest bidders.

You are probably familiar with the story from here. Crammed into the holds of ships to the point where they could only sit or lay, thousands died on the long voyage to the New World. Others, chained together, threw themselves overboard before the evil slave ships ever set sail. Enough survived, however, to make the slave trade a profitable business for those engaged in it.

A small number of Africans brought to the New World were purchased and made household slaves. These were the lucky ones. The vast majority ended up laboring on plantations either in the south or on Portuguese and Spanish sugar, rice, and cotton plantations in Latin America and the West Indies. Many others toiled away in Spanish gold and silver mines.

The first blacks from Africa arrive at Jamestown in 1619. Although they were sold as indentured servants, blacks would later be auctioned off as slaves.

From *Everyday Life: Exploration and Discovery* © 2005 Good Year Books.

The beginning of the slave trade in the Western Hemisphere was a negative consequence of the Age of Exploration and Discovery. Most results, however, were of a positive nature, especially with regard to Europe. The period of exploration brought on an economic or commercial revolution throughout the continent. All remaining vestiges (traces) of the Middle Ages came to an end and a new age began.

One change that affected Europe was the increased availability of money. You may recall from chapter 4 that during the Middle Ages gold deposits were used up and the silver mines of Germany could not meet the demand for metal with which to make coins. But with gold and silver pouring into the continent from mines in Mexico and Peru, there was no shortage of metals. As a result, barter ended completely and coined money became widespread.

With more money in circulation, there was a need for banks in which to keep it. Thus, the growth of the banking industry was another result of exploration. Banks were also needed to provide the capital

necessary to establish new businesses and to finance more exploration and colonization efforts. The extension of credit and payment by check was also a boon to industrial expansion. Partly because of the banking industry, a new, prosperous middle class consisting of merchants, bankers, and businessmen began to take its place in European politics and society.

Monarchs also benefited from the greater availability of money. With more money in circulation, they could collect more taxes. This in turn made it possible for them to increase the size of their armies and navies, thereby further weakening the power of the nobles and aiding the cause of national unity.

Another change brought on by the Age of Exploration and Discovery was a shift of the world's commercial center from the Mediterranean to the Atlantic. Great cities such as London, Lisbon, Antwerp, and Amsterdam became great

Increased use of money led to the appearance of more moneychangers like these men. Moneychangers changed the metal coins of one country for those of another.

ocean ports. Previously, the Italian city-states of Genoa and Venice had held a monopoly on trade. These cities, located far from the Atlantic Ocean, now declined in importance.

Nowhere was the impact of exploration more apparent than in the introduction of new foods and products. For the first time people dined on corn, pumpkins, potatoes, squash, chili peppers, rice, and turkey. They drank coffee from the Middle East and the Spice Islands, cocoa from America, and tea from China and India. These were made even more enjoyable because of an abundant supply of sugar coming in from plantations in the West Indies. The arrival of new drinks led to the growth of coffeehouses, tearooms, and chocolate shops, where people gathered and shared opinions about politics and other subjects. While so engaged, many indulged in another recently introduced product: tobacco.

In the 1500s and 1600s, products that had been rare and exotic became more available to people with means. Furs from North America were worn by the upper classes, and furniture made from fine West Indian cedar and mahogany adorned their homes. On their hats they sported ostrich feathers from Africa, and above their heads they carried decorative umbrellas from Asia. They also enjoyed Asian fans, gems, porcelain, spices, silks, wallpaper, and perfumes. Such products could be only dreamed of during the Middle Ages.

The race for overseas possessions created tensions between rival European powers. The Dutch seized Portuguese trading posts in the East Indies, while the English came into conflict with the Dutch, French, and Spanish in the Americas. In time, the English drove both the Dutch and the French out of North America.

The English confrontation with the Spanish is worthy of note because it helped hasten Spain's decline as a major power. It began with the raiding activities of English privateers. Privateers were privately owned vessels sailing in the service of the English Crown. Commanded by such swashbuckling sea captains as Sir John Hawkins and Sir Francis Drake, they were, in effect, pirate ships, but they were pirate ships operating with the blessing of Queen Elizabeth I. In the years following Spain's conquest of Mexico and Peru, English privateers preyed on gold-laden Spanish galleons on their way to Europe. They also attacked and raided Spanish settlements in the New World. Such attacks resulted in a large amount of Spanish gold and silver finding its way into England's royal treasury.

From *Everyday Life: Exploration and Discovery* © 2005 Good Year Books.

By 1588, tension between Spain and England resulted in war. King Philip II of Spain, incensed at his rival not only for their raids on his ships but because they were Protestant, sent a large fleet of warships to invade and conquer England. This large fleet was the Spanish Armada. It consisted of 130 warships and more than 8,000 sailors. The ships were armed with some 2,500 cannon and could carry as many as 29,000 soldiers for the land invasion. With such a formidable force, Philip was certain he could defeat the English.

But it was not to be. Met in the English Channel by a fleet of smaller, faster, English vessels, the Spanish galleons suffered a devastating defeat. Many of those that managed to escape were destroyed a few days later in a great storm. With the destruction of its armada, Spanish sea power declined and England became master of the seas. Never again would Spain be considered a major European power after its crushing naval defeat of 1588.

Ships of the Spanish Armada. The defeat of the Armada in 1588 saved England from invasion and led to the decline of Spain.

Another result of exploration was that the discovery of new lands stimulated science. During the Middle Ages, science and medicine were dominated by superstition. Many people believed, for example, that witches flew through the air and that the juice of lizards rubbed on cuts brought immediate relief. These same people also had faith that magic potions and magic charms would guarantee good luck, fend off devils, and bring about other desired results. Such superstitions waned, however, in light of the increased knowledge of geography, zoology, botany, and astronomy brought about by direct contact with other lands and other peoples.

Finally, wherever explorers and colonizers went, they took with them their culture and their religion. Missionaries accompanied expeditions, and, through their efforts, large numbers of the native populations in the New World and elsewhere were converted to Christianity.

Name _____ Date _____

Make a Mobile

You learned in chapter 11 that many new foods and products found their way to Europe as a result of the Age of Exploration and Discovery. With a few simple materials, you can make a mobile depicting some of these goods.

To make a more detailed mobile, cut pieces of stiff wire in lengths of about six inches. Slightly bend each piece in the middle to give it a rainbow shape. Attach a cut-out to each end of the wire strips. Tie different lengths of string to the middle of the pieces of wire and then hang the strips from the bottom of the clothes hanger.

Here Is What You Will Need:

1. Large clothes hanger
2. Construction paper or small index cards
3. Crayons or coloring pencils
4. Felt-tipped pen
5. Hole punch
6. String
7. Some stiff wire (optional)

Here Is What You Do:

1. Cut construction paper or index cards to sizes of about 2" by 3". If you prefer, cut some in the shape of rectangles, squares, triangles, and so on.

2. Write the name of a food or some other product on the front of each cut-out.

3. On the back of each, write the region of the world from which the product came.

4. Punch a hole at the top of each cut-out.

5. Insert and tie a piece of string through the hole at the top of each cut-out. Make your pieces of string different lengths so you can stagger the cut-outs on the clothes hanger.

6. Attach each card or cut-out to the bottom of the clothes hanger.

7. Make a sign reading "New Foods and Products," and attach it to the top of the hanger.

From Everyday Life: Exploration and Discovery © 2005 GoodYear Books.

Name _____ Date _____

Rank the Results of Exploration and Discovery

Read back over the changes brought about by the Age of Exploration and Discovery. Then, on the lines provided, list in order the three changes you consider the most important. Explain in detail why you chose each of the three.

1. _____
_____
_____
_____
_____
_____
_____
_____

2. _____
_____
_____
_____
_____
_____
_____
_____

3. _____
_____
_____
_____
_____
_____
_____

Name _____ Date _____

Rewrite a Part of History

Suppose slavery had never taken hold in the New World. How do you think history might have turned out differently? Would large plantations have risen in the South? Would there have been a U.S. Civil War?

On the lines provided, tell how you think such a scenario might have altered the history of our nation.

From Everyday Life: Exploration and Discovery © 2005 Good Year Books.

Name _____ Date _____

Make an Outline

Using correct form (Roman numeral, capital letter, Arabic numeral, lowercase letter, and proper punctuation and indentation), make a topic outline of the highlights of the Age of Exploration and Discovery. Broad topics—those listed next to Roman numerals—have been done for you.

Look back through all the chapters for help in completing your outline.

I. Early Explorations

_____

_____

_____

_____

_____

II. Factors Bringing on the Great Age of Discovery

_____

_____

_____

_____

_____

III. Conquests and Colonies of Rival Powers

_____

_____

_____

_____

IV. Effects of Exploration and Discovery

_____

_____

_____

_____

_____

Everyday Life: Exploration and Discovery

Answers to Activities

Chapter 1
Name Those Explorers
1. Minoans 2. Phoenicians 3. Herodotus
4. General Hanno 5. Herodotus
6. Alexander the Great 7. Hippalus 8. Romans
9. Eric the Red 10. Vikings 11. Leif Ericson
12. Leif Ericson 13. Romans

Use Your Critical-Thinking Skills
Answers will vary.

Brush Up on Your Geography
1. Greece; Canea 2. Middle East; Beirut;
Damascus 3. Iraq; Baghdad 4. Persia; Teheran (or
Tehran) 5. Sri Lanka; Colombo 6. Hanoi
7. Godthaab 8. Canada; St. Johns

Chapter 2
Make False Statements True
1. Cathay 2. Venice 3. uncle 4. 17 5. four
6. Persia 7. Mongolia 8. Ceylon 9. Myanmar
10. Peking 11. paper money 12. Persia 13. Genoa

Name Those Synonyms and Antonyms
The following are possible answers:
1. effective; ineffective 2. prod; dissuade
3. unlikely; believable 4. left; arrived
5. joyous; displeased 6. splendid; plain
7. rarely; frequently 8. correct; wrong
9. uncurving; crooked 10. hard; easy
11. profit; disadvantage 12. capable; incompetent
13. took; rejected 14. valuable; worthless
15. join; abandon 16. complete; empty
17. finished; started 18. huge; small
19. satisfied; displeased 20. meekness; vanity

Chapter 3
Do Research on Scurvy
1. A disease caused by the lack of vitamin C in
   the diet
2. Swollen and soft, bleeding gums, often resulting
   in loss of teeth; anemia; tired feeling; swelling of
   the joints
3. They usually subsisted on a diet of hardtack
   and salt beef.

4. Scurvy is prevented by adding foods rich in
   vitamin C to the diet. It can be treated through
   doses of ascorbic acid.
5. Because they were giving a daily ration of lime
   juice to prevent scurvy

Distinguish between Sentences and Fragments
1. F 2. S 3. F 4. S 5. F 6. F 7. S 8. F 9. S
Sentences will vary.

Chapter 4
Identify Those Spices
Answers should contain one of each of the
following examples:
1. puddings, preserves, relishes 2. candies, cookies,
pastry, sweet pickles 3. meats, tomato dishes
4. soups, stews, sauces, pickling 5. chili con carne,
Mexican foods 6. candies, baked goods
7. desserts, candies, soups 8. curry and chili
powders 9. gingerbread, gingersnaps, cakes
10. dressings, soups, stews, vegetables
11. fish, soup, stews, sauces 12. prepared mustard,
pickling, meats, sauces 13. puddings, eggnog, baking
14. Italian foods, such as pizza 15. garnish on
combination meat and vegetable dishes
16. garnish on meat dishes and salads
17. seasoning for meats and vegetables
18. sausages, cheese, sauces 19. bread toppings
20. chowders, stews, stuffings

Fill in a Venn Diagram
Answers will vary but should be similar to the
following:
Age of Exploration: improved navigation was made
possible by the compass, the astrolabe, and better-
made ships;
Both: adventuresome, exciting, and explorations of
unknown worlds; certain risks and dangers
involved with each;
Exploration of Space: advanced technology, means of
travel, and a more exact knowledge of the universe.

Complete a Vocabulary Exercise
1. a 2. c 3. b 4. a 5. b 6. c 7. a

90

From Everyday Life: Exploration and Discovery © 2005 Good Year Books.